Walking Through Walls God's Power to Part the Storms of Life

Joshua Rhoades

Published by Joshua Paul Rhoades, 2024.

WALKING THROUGH WALLS GOD'S POWER TO PART THE STORMS OF LIFE

First edition. September 21, 2024.

Copyright © 2024 Joshua Rhoades.

ISBN: 979-8227134240

Written by Joshua Rhoades.

Also by Joshua Rhoades

Courage Under Fire: David's Stand On The Battlefield
Jonah's Journey: Voices Of Redemption And Lessons In Obedience
The Furnace Of Faith: 12 Principles From The Heat Of Faith
Whispers of Hope: Inspiring Stories of Men's Prayers In Scripture
Frontier Legends: The Oregon Dream
Elijah: A Beacon Of Boldness
HOOK, LINE & SAVIOUR - Faith Reflections from Fishing
Driven By Faith: Motor Racing Inspired Christian Life
30 Day Devotional - Bold and Strong- Coffee Devotions for a Courageous Christian Walk
Authentic Christianity: The Heart of Old Time Religion
Consider The Ant - God's Tiny Preachers
Flee Fornication: The Plea For Purity
Renewed Hope- How to Find Encouragement in God
Sounding The Call - The Voice of Conviction
The Altar - Where Heaven Meets Earth
The Bible's Battlefields- Timeless Lessons from Ancient Wars
The Sacred Art of Silence - How Silence Speaks in Scripture
Under Fire- The Sanctity of the Traditional Biblical Home
Who Is on the Lord's Side? A Call to Righteousness
What Is Truth? - From Skepticism to Submission
First and Goal- Faith and Football Fundamentals
From Dugout to Devotion- Spiritual Lessons from Baseball
Par for the Course- Faith and Fairways
The Believer's Pace- Tools for Running Life's Marathon
The Immutable Fortress- Security in God's Unchanging Nature
Biblical Bravery
Deer Stands and Devotions: A Hunter's Walk with God

Dedication

To you, dear reader,

This book, "Walking Through Walls: God's Power to Part the Storms of Life," is dedicated to your unwavering desire to grow in your walk with the Lord. Your choice to open these pages, to seek wisdom and understanding in the midst of life's challenges, speaks to the depth of your faith and your longing to experience the power of God in a more profound way. It takes courage to confront the storms of life, and it takes even more faith to trust that God is there, ready to part the seas before you. You have shown that courage and that faith simply by embarking on this journey.

Life brings walls that seem insurmountable—barriers that stand in the way of the peace, purpose, and progress we seek. But your willingness to learn, to dive into Scripture, and to trust in God's promises is a testament to your heart's desire to walk closely with Him, no matter the circumstances. You have chosen not to give up, not to allow fear, doubt, or uncertainty to overwhelm you. Instead, you have chosen to seek God's guidance, His presence, and His power to overcome whatever challenges may lie ahead.

This book is for you—the one who seeks to deepen your understanding of God's miraculous intervention in life's most difficult moments. The lessons learned in Exodus 14 are not just stories of ancient times; they are timeless truths that continue to apply to every believer today. As you read and reflect, my hope is that you will see the hand of God more clearly in your own life, that you will be reminded that no wall, no storm, and no challenge is too great for the God you serve.

You are here because you desire to grow, to trust God in ways that you perhaps never have before. You are seeking a faith that isn't shaken by the trials of life but strengthened by them. And this desire is something that pleases God deeply. Hebrews 11:6 reminds us that "without faith, it is impossible to please Him," and you are already walking in faith simply by pursuing Him in these moments of uncertainty. You are stepping out, much like the Israelites did, trusting that God will make a way even when you cannot see it.

May this book be a source of encouragement, a reminder that God is with you in every trial, and a testament to the fact that He is still in the business of parting seas, moving mountains, and walking through walls. Your journey is not in vain. Every step you take toward God, every moment you spend seeking His will, is a step toward transformation, growth, and spiritual maturity.

I dedicate this book to you because your desire to walk with the Lord is the first step in experiencing His power. As you read, I pray that your heart will be stirred, your faith will be strengthened, and your relationship with God will deepen in ways you never imagined. May you be inspired to keep walking, keep trusting, and keep believing that with God, all things truly are possible.

With faith and gratitude for your journey,

Joshua Rhoades

Introduction

In life, we all face moments when we feel trapped, like there's no way out, and the obstacles in front of us seem impossible to overcome. These challenges can be overwhelming—whether it's financial struggles, broken relationships, health crises, or personal failures. In those moments, it feels like we're standing at the edge of a sea with no way forward, much like the Israelites found themselves at the Red Sea, with the Egyptian army bearing down on them and the waters standing as an impassable barrier. But just as God parted the Red Sea, creating a path of deliverance for His people, He can part the storms in our lives and make a way where there seems to be no way. In "Walking Through Walls: God's Power to Part the Storms of Life", we will explore the incredible story of God's intervention at the Red Sea from Exodus 14, and the lessons it holds for us today. This miraculous event wasn't just about God's power over nature; it was about His unwavering faithfulness to His people, His timing, and His ability to turn impossible situations into opportunities for His glory. Throughout this book, we'll dive deep into how God works in our lives through trials and obstacles, using them as a means of drawing us closer to Him. We'll explore how faith, obedience, patience, and trust in God's timing are key to experiencing His power in the midst of our storms. Just as God provided a way for the Israelites when all hope seemed lost, He is ready to do the same for you. The walls you're facing right now—the barriers that seem too high, the waves that look too strong—are no match for God's power. He is the God who makes the impossible possible. As you read this book, be prepared to see how God can work in your life, even in your most desperate moments. The Red Sea was more than just a story of deliverance; it was a declaration of God's ability to turn obstacles into opportunities for miracles. It's a reminder that when you trust God and walk in faith, He will lead you through the impossible, walking through walls that once seemed impenetrable. You'll learn how God's power, presence, and timing come together to deliver His people, and how these truths apply to the storms you face today. Whether you're going through a season of uncertainty, fear, or struggle, this book will guide you to a deeper trust in God's ability to part the waters and lead you to victory. Like the Israelites, you too can walk through walls, not by your own strength, but by the power of the God who goes before you, making a way through the storms of life. Let this journey of faith inspire you to keep trusting, keep walking, and keep believing that with God, all things are possible.

Chapter 1 - Wait on God's Timing

In Exodus 14:21-22, 26-27, we see one of the most powerful moments in the Bible when God intervenes for His people in a seemingly impossible situation. The Israelites, having fled from slavery in Egypt, found themselves trapped between the Red Sea and the approaching Egyptian army. With no way forward and their enemies closing in, it must have felt like they were out of options. Fear gripped the hearts of the people as they saw the chariots coming closer, and they began to cry out in despair, questioning whether leaving Egypt had been the right choice. But in that moment, God was still in control, and He was about to demonstrate His power and faithfulness in a way they could have never imagined. Moses told the people to "stand still and see the salvation of the Lord" (Exodus 14:13), and with a mighty hand, God commanded Moses to stretch out his rod over the sea. At the perfect moment, God caused a strong east wind to blow all night, parting the waters and creating a dry path for the Israelites to walk through. This miraculous event didn't just showcase God's power over nature; it revealed a critical lesson about waiting on God's timing. Even when it seemed like time had run out, when the Israelites felt completely cornered and without hope, God showed up at exactly the right moment. He knew when to act, and His timing was flawless.

Waiting on God's timing is something we all struggle with, especially when we're facing our own "Red Sea moments." When we are in difficult circumstances, it's natural to want immediate solutions, quick fixes, and instant relief. But what we learn from the parting of the Red Sea is that God's timing is not always our timing. We might feel like we are at the end of the road, with no way out and no options left, but that doesn't mean God isn't working behind the scenes. The Israelites had no idea that God was about to split the sea; they only saw the waves and the enemy. In the same way, we often can't see what God is preparing for us when we are in the middle of our trials. It's easy to become anxious, fearful, or frustrated when the answers we seek aren't immediately clear. But the story of the Red Sea reminds us that even when we can't see the solution, God already knows the perfect moment to intervene. He waits until the precise time when His power will be displayed most clearly and when our faith will be strengthened the most.

The key to waiting on God's timing is trust. Just as the Israelites had to trust that Moses was leading them correctly, even when it didn't seem logical, we must trust that God knows what He's doing, even when we don't understand His plan. In Exodus 14:14, Moses reassured the people, saying, "The Lord shall fight for you, and ye shall hold your peace." This is a powerful statement that reminds us that sometimes, the best thing we can do is to be still and trust in God's ability to work on our behalf. Waiting is not a passive activity; it's an active expression of faith. It means believing that God is at work, even when we don't see it yet, and knowing that His plans for us are good. The Israelites had to wait as the wind blew and the waters were parted. They had to walk in faith through the path God created, trusting that the walls of water wouldn't collapse on them. This teaches us that waiting on God often requires us to take steps of faith, even when the situation still seems uncertain. We might not know how things will work out, but we can trust that God will lead us through safely, just as He led the Israelites.

Another important aspect of waiting on God's timing is learning patience. Patience is one of the hardest virtues to develop, especially when we feel the pressure of time running out. The Israelites were panicking as they saw the Egyptians closing in, and it's easy to understand why. Their fear was real, and the threat was imminent. But God wasn't rushed by their anxiety or pressured by the urgency of the situation. He had a plan all along, and He knew exactly when to part the sea. In our own lives, we often want God to move faster, to solve our problems right away, and to remove our difficulties instantly. But God's timing is perfect, and His delays are not denials. Sometimes, He allows us to stay in a difficult situation longer than we would like because He is developing something in us—whether it's patience, faith, perseverance, or a deeper understanding of His character. The Israelites needed to learn to trust God fully, not just when things were going well, but even when they were in a desperate situation. We, too, are called to develop this kind of trust, where we believe that God's timing is always best, even when it seems like He's taking too long.

Waiting on God's timing also teaches us to let go of our own control. The Israelites had no control over their situation. They couldn't fight the Egyptian army, and they couldn't part the Red Sea on their own. All they could do was wait for God to act. This is often where we struggle the most—letting go of our desire to control the outcome and instead surrendering to God's will. We want to fix things ourselves, to find our own solutions, and to take matters into our own hands. But the Red Sea moment teaches us that there are some situations that only God can handle, and we need to step back and let Him take over. When we try to force our own solutions, we often end up making things worse or delaying the blessing that God has prepared for us. But when we wait on God, trusting that He knows what's best, we open ourselves up to experiencing His miracles in ways we never could have imagined.

Another key lesson from the parting of the Red Sea is that God's timing often involves testing our faith. The Israelites were in a vulnerable position, and their faith was being tested. Would they trust God, or would they give in to fear? Would they wait for His deliverance, or would they try to find their own way out? Waiting on God's timing often puts our faith to the test because it forces us to rely on Him completely. It's in these moments of waiting that our faith is stretched and strengthened. The Israelites had to believe that God would make a way where there was no way. They had to trust that the waters wouldn't collapse as they walked through the sea. In the same way, when we are waiting on God's timing, we are called to walk in faith, believing that He will come through for us, even when the situation seems impossible.

The parting of the Red Sea also teaches us that God's timing is not just about our deliverance—it's about His glory. When God finally acted and parted the sea, it was a miraculous display of His power and majesty. The Egyptians, who had been pursuing the Israelites, were utterly defeated when the waters came crashing down on them. In Exodus 14:17-18, God said, "And I, behold, I will harden the hearts of the Egyptians, and they shall follow them: and I will get me honour upon Pharaoh, and upon all his host, upon his chariots, and upon his horsemen. And the Egyptians shall know that I am the Lord." God's timing was perfect because it not only saved the Israelites, but it also showed the Egyptians and the surrounding nations that He alone was God. When we wait on God's timing, we can trust that He is not only working for our good, but also for His glory. He wants to demonstrate His power and His faithfulness in our lives in ways that will draw others to Him. When we are patient and wait for God to act, He often uses our testimony to inspire and encourage others who are facing their own storms.

Finally, waiting on God's timing reminds us that His deliverance is always worth the wait. The Israelites were delivered from an impossible situation, and their lives were forever changed. They experienced firsthand the power and faithfulness of God, and their trust in Him was deepened. When we wait on God, we can be confident that His deliverance will be greater than anything we could have imagined. The Red Sea wasn't just a way of escape; it was a path to freedom, a demonstration of God's covenant with His people, and a foreshadowing of the ultimate deliverance that would come through Jesus Christ. When we wait on God's timing, we are not just waiting for a solution to our problems—we are waiting for God to reveal His plan, to strengthen our faith, and to draw us closer to Him.

In conclusion, the story of the parting of the Red Sea in Exodus 14:21-22, 26-27 is a powerful lesson in waiting on God's timing. The Israelites were trapped and out of options, but God acted at the perfect moment, showing that His timing is always flawless. Waiting on God requires trust, patience, and a willingness to surrender our own control. It tests our faith and teaches us to rely completely on His power and His plan. God's timing is not just about our deliverance—it's about His glory, and when we wait on Him, we can be confident that His deliverance will be worth the wait. The Red Sea moment reminds us that no matter how impossible our circumstances may seem, God can part the waters and lead us through to freedom, if only we are willing to wait on His perfect timing.

Chapter 2 - Wind and Wonder of God

In Exodus 14:21-22, 26-27, we witness one of the most miraculous and awe-inspiring moments in the Bible, where God displayed His supreme authority over nature by parting the Red Sea. As the Israelites found themselves trapped between the vast, seemingly impassable waters of the Red Sea and the advancing Egyptian army, fear gripped their hearts. They were in a dire situation, unable to move forward or retreat. But God, in His power and sovereignty, intervened in a way no one could have anticipated. In Exodus 14:21, we read, "And Moses stretched out his hand over the sea; and the Lord caused the sea to go back by a strong east wind all that night, and made the sea dry land, and the waters were divided." Here, God used the wind—something as invisible and unpredictable as the air—to accomplish a feat that was beyond human comprehension. The wind that God sent was not just a breeze, but a powerful force that split the sea in two, creating a path of dry land for the Israelites to cross safely. This act of God's wind and wonder is a reminder of His omnipotence and His ability to work in ways that defy logic and natural order. God is not limited by the constraints of the physical world. He can command the wind, the seas, and all of creation to accomplish His purposes, and this moment at the Red Sea stands as a testament to His unmatched power and ability to intervene in impossible situations.

The use of the wind in this story is significant because it illustrates how God can take something that seems ordinary and transform it into a vehicle for His extraordinary purposes. Wind is a natural phenomenon that we experience in our daily lives, yet in this instance, God used it in a supernatural way. The wind was His instrument to part the waters, demonstrating that even the most mundane elements of creation are subject to His will. This teaches us that God can use anything, no matter how ordinary or insignificant it may seem, to bring about His wonders. Whether it's the wind, water, or other elements of nature, God's power is limitless, and He can turn the most unlikely things into channels of His miraculous works. This is a powerful reminder that God is always at work, even in ways we don't always recognize. The same God who commanded the wind to part the Red Sea can use the seemingly ordinary things in our lives to bring about extraordinary outcomes. We often expect God to work in grand, visible ways, but He frequently chooses to use subtle, yet powerful, means to achieve His purposes.

God's use of the wind in Exodus 14:21 also reminds us of His timing and precision. The Bible says that the wind blew all night, steadily parting the waters and drying the land beneath. This wasn't a sudden, instantaneous event, but rather a process that unfolded according to God's perfect timing. The Israelites had to wait through the night as the wind did its work, but in the morning, they saw the results of God's wondrous intervention. This teaches us that while we may not always see the full picture of what God is doing in the moment, He is always at work behind the scenes. Like the wind that parted the sea, God's work in our lives can be gradual and sometimes imperceptible, but it is always purposeful and effective. We must trust that God's timing is perfect, and that even when we don't see immediate results, He is working all things together for our good. Just as the Israelites awoke to find a clear path through the sea, we too will see the fruits of God's work in our lives if we are patient and trust in His process.

The wonder of this miracle is not only in the parting of the sea but in the fact that God chose to make the path through the waters completely dry. Exodus 14:22 tells us, "And the children of Israel went into the midst of the sea upon the dry ground: and the waters were a wall unto them on their right hand, and on their left." The ground beneath the sea, which had been covered by water for centuries, was instantly dried by the wind. This is a profound detail that underscores the completeness of God's miracles. He didn't just make a way through the sea; He made the way safe, stable, and secure for the Israelites to walk on. The walls of water on either side of them were a visual representation of God's power holding back the forces of nature, allowing His people to pass through unharmed. This teaches us that when God makes a way for us, He does so thoroughly and perfectly. He doesn't just provide partial solutions or temporary fixes; He provides complete deliverance, ensuring that every step we take is on solid ground. When God intervenes in our lives, He does so in a way that leaves no room for doubt about His power and care.

Another important aspect of this miracle is that God used the same waters that He parted to bring judgment upon the Egyptians. In Exodus 14:26-27, God commanded Moses to stretch out his hand over the sea once more, and the waters returned to their place, covering the Egyptians who had pursued the Israelites into the sea. This dual aspect of the miracle—deliverance for the Israelites and destruction for the Egyptians—reveals God's justice and His ability to use the same forces of nature for both salvation and judgment. The same wind that parted the sea for God's people became the means of their enemies' downfall. This teaches us that God's power is both protective and purifying. He can use the very obstacles in our lives as tools to defeat our enemies and bring about our deliverance. The Egyptians had trusted in their own strength and military might, but they were no match for the power of God's wind and wonder. This moment demonstrates that those who oppose God's people ultimately face His justice, and no force of evil can withstand His mighty hand.

The parting of the Red Sea is also a profound example of God's faithfulness to His promises. God had promised to deliver the Israelites from slavery in Egypt, and He fulfilled that promise in a way that no one could have predicted. The Israelites had no way of knowing that God would use the wind to part the sea, but He did so to show them—and future generations—that His promises are sure and that He is always faithful. This miracle was a turning point in the Israelites' journey, a moment when they saw God's power and faithfulness on full display. It teaches us that God is always faithful to His word, and He often fulfills His promises in ways that exceed our expectations. When we face challenges or seemingly impossible situations, we can hold onto the assurance that God is faithful and will make a way, even if we can't see how. His wind and wonder are always at work, often in ways that are beyond our comprehension, but always in line with His promises.

Furthermore, the parting of the Red Sea serves as a powerful reminder that God works wonders for the sake of His people. The Israelites were not a powerful nation; they were former slaves fleeing from a dominant empire. Yet, God chose to intervene on their behalf, showing that His wonders are not reserved for the powerful or the mighty, but for those who trust in Him. This teaches us that God's miracles are not based on our strength or status, but on His love and care for us. He delights in working wonders in the lives of those who rely on Him, and He is always ready to demonstrate His power when we are in need. The parting of the Red Sea is a reminder that God is not distant or uninvolved in the struggles of His people. He sees our needs, hears our cries, and responds with power and wonder, just as He did for the Israelites.

The wind and wonder of God at the Red Sea also highlight His ability to bring order out of chaos. The sea, which represented chaos and danger for the Israelites, was transformed into a pathway of deliverance by God's command. This teaches us that God can bring order and peace to the most chaotic and turbulent situations in our lives. Just as He parted the waters and created a clear path for the Israelites, He can bring clarity and direction to our lives when we are overwhelmed by confusion or uncertainty. God is not intimidated by chaos; in fact, He specializes in bringing order out of it. The same wind that parted the waters can blow away the confusion and fear that often cloud our judgment, allowing us to see the path that God has prepared for us.

In conclusion, the parting of the Red Sea in Exodus 14:21-22, 26-27 is a profound demonstration of God's wind and wonder. Through a powerful east wind, God parted the waters, creating a dry path for the Israelites to walk through, and ultimately bringing judgment upon their enemies. This miracle teaches us that God's power over nature is limitless, and He can use the elements of creation to accomplish His purposes in ways we could never predict. It reminds us to trust in God's timing, to have faith in His ability to deliver us, and to recognize that even in the midst of impossible situations, God is always at work, bringing about His wonders. Whether we are facing personal challenges, fears, or obstacles that seem insurmountable, we can find comfort and hope in the knowledge that the same God who parted the Red Sea is with us today. He can part the waters in our lives, turning chaos into order, fear into faith, and obstacles into pathways for His glory. God's wind and wonder are always at work, and we are called to trust in His power, knowing that He is able to do far more than we could ever ask or imagine.

Chapter 3 - Withstand Fear With Faith

In Exodus 14:21-22, 26-27, we see one of the most dramatic moments in the Bible unfold. The Israelites, having just escaped the oppressive rule of Egypt, find themselves trapped between the Red Sea and the Egyptian army. The Egyptian forces, with their powerful chariots and soldiers, were closing in, and the sea lay before the Israelites, seemingly blocking their path to freedom. Fear spread quickly through the camp as they realized their precarious position. Many began to question whether they had made the right choice in leaving Egypt. They felt cornered, helpless, and out of options. In that moment, panic could easily have overtaken them. However, Moses, their leader, gave them a powerful command: "Fear ye not, stand still, and see the salvation of the Lord, which He will show to you today" (Exodus 14:13). Moses encouraged them to withstand their fear with faith, urging them to trust in God's plan even when the situation seemed hopeless. This scene teaches us a timeless lesson about the importance of relying on our faith to withstand fear, especially when facing overwhelming challenges. The Israelites, though filled with anxiety, were called to trust in God's ability to deliver them, even when they couldn't see a way out. Their story reminds us that, no matter how terrifying our circumstances may seem, we can stand firm and trust that God is in control, and He has a plan for our deliverance.

Fear is a natural human response to danger or uncertainty, and the Israelites had every reason to be afraid from a human perspective. The Egyptian army was known for its might and strength, and the Israelites were not warriors—they were former slaves who had spent generations in bondage. They had no military training or weapons to defend themselves, and they were facing a formidable enemy. It's easy to imagine how fear gripped their hearts as they saw the dust from the approaching chariots and heard the thunderous roar of the army behind them. They were in a situation where fear seemed like the only logical response. Yet, Moses reminded them that they were not alone. He called them to stand still and trust in God's power, to resist the urge to flee in panic or give up in despair. In essence, Moses was telling the Israelites that while fear was understandable, it wasn't necessary, because God was with them. This moment teaches us that faith doesn't mean we will never feel fear; rather, it means that we choose to trust God even in the presence of fear. When fear threatens to overwhelm us, we must remember that God is greater than any obstacle we face, and His power is more than sufficient to carry us through.

Faith is not the absence of fear, but the decision to trust God despite our fears. The Israelites had to make a choice in that moment: would they allow fear to paralyze them, or would they choose to have faith in God's promises? Moses reminded them that God had already delivered them from Egypt, and that same God would continue to guide and protect them. The Red Sea may have seemed like an insurmountable barrier, but God had a plan that was greater than anything they could have imagined. This teaches us that, in times of fear, we must look back on God's faithfulness in our lives and remember how He has brought us through previous trials. When we reflect on God's past deliverances, our faith is strengthened, and we can face our current challenges with greater confidence. Just as God parted the Red Sea for the Israelites, He is able to make a way for us through whatever obstacles we are facing. The key is to stand firm in faith and trust that God is working, even when we can't see the solution.

Moses' command to "stand still" is particularly powerful. In moments of fear, our natural instinct is often to react quickly, to try to fix the situation ourselves, or to run away from the problem. But Moses urged the Israelites to do the opposite. He told them to stand still and watch what God would do. This teaches us an important lesson about waiting on God's timing and resisting the urge to take matters into our own hands. Standing still doesn't mean doing nothing—it means placing our full trust in God and allowing Him to work on our behalf. When we are faced with overwhelming fear, we must resist the temptation to act out of panic or desperation. Instead, we must stand firm in our faith, knowing that God is fighting for us. The Israelites had to trust that God would make a way, even though they couldn't see how. This is the essence of faith—believing in God's power and goodness, even when the situation seems impossible. By standing still, the Israelites were not giving up; they were choosing to trust in the only One who could truly deliver them.

The parting of the Red Sea in Exodus 14:21-22 is a vivid demonstration of God's power over nature and His ability to intervene in the most extraordinary ways. The Israelites had no idea that God was about to part the sea; all they saw was the impossible situation in front of them. But God used a strong east wind to divide the waters, creating a path of dry land for His people to walk through. This miraculous event shows us that God can work in ways we could never predict or imagine. When we are trapped by fear and can't see a way out, God is already working behind the scenes, preparing a way for us. The Israelites' fear was real, but God's power was greater. This reminds us that, no matter how daunting our circumstances may be, God is always in control, and He can make a way where there seems to be no way. The sea, which seemed like an insurmountable barrier, became the very thing God used to deliver His people and destroy their enemies. This teaches us that the things we fear the most can become the very tools God uses to bring about our victory. When we place our faith in God, He can turn our greatest fears into our greatest triumphs.

Exodus 14:26-27 further illustrates how God's power extends not only to deliverance but also to justice. After the Israelites had crossed the sea, God instructed Moses to stretch out his hand once more, and the waters returned, covering the Egyptian army and drowning them. The same sea that had been a path of deliverance for the Israelites became a grave for their enemies. This shows us that God is not only our deliverer but also our defender. He fights our battles for us, and we can trust Him to bring justice in His time and in His way. The Egyptians had pursued the Israelites with the intention of capturing or killing them, but God's plan was greater. He used the very thing they thought would trap the Israelites—the sea—to defeat them. This teaches us that when we face opposition or danger, we don't need to fear because God is our protector. He sees what we are going through, and He will act on our behalf when the time is right. Our job is to trust Him and have faith that He is working, even when we don't understand how.

Faith also requires us to step into the unknown. When the Israelites began to cross the Red Sea, they had to walk between two walls of water, trusting that the waters would not collapse on them. This was a significant act of faith. They had never seen anything like this before, and they didn't know how long the waters would remain parted. But they stepped forward in faith, trusting that God would keep them safe. This teaches us that faith often requires us to step out, even when we can't see the full picture. When God calls us to move forward, we must do so with the confidence that He will sustain us. The path may seem uncertain, and the risks may feel overwhelming, but when we trust in God's plan, we can walk forward with faith, knowing that He will guide us every step of the way. The Israelites' faith allowed them to walk through the sea to safety, and it is our faith that allows us to navigate the storms and challenges of life.

One of the most comforting aspects of this story is the reminder that God sees our fear and responds with compassion and power. The Israelites were terrified, and yet God did not condemn them for their fear. Instead, He provided a way for them to overcome it by displaying His power and faithfulness. This teaches us that God understands our fears and meets us in our moments of weakness. He doesn't expect us to be fearless; He simply asks us to trust Him and rely on His strength. When we bring our fears to God, He gives us the faith we need to withstand them. He doesn't leave us to face our fears alone—He walks with us, fights for us, and ultimately delivers us from the very things we are afraid of.

In conclusion, Exodus 14:21-22, 26-27 teaches us a profound lesson about withstanding fear with faith. The Israelites, though terrified by their circumstances, were called to trust in God's plan and stand firm in their faith. Moses' command to "stand still" reminds us that in moments of fear, we must resist the urge to panic or act impulsively. Instead, we are called to place our trust in God and allow Him to work on our behalf. The parting of the Red Sea demonstrates that God's power is greater than any obstacle we face and that He can deliver us in ways we could never imagine. Faith doesn't mean the absence of fear—it means trusting God in the midst of fear and believing that He is in control. Just as the Israelites were delivered from their enemies and brought safely through the sea, we too can trust that God will deliver us from whatever challenges we face. Our faith in God's plan allows us to withstand fear and walk forward in confidence, knowing that He is with us every step of the way.

Chapter 4 - Willingness to Obey Brings Wonders

In Exodus 14:21-22, 26-27, one of the most awe-inspiring and pivotal moments in biblical history takes place as Moses, by God's command, stretches out his hand over the Red Sea, and the waters miraculously part, allowing the Israelites to escape from the pursuing Egyptian army. This event is not only a demonstration of God's immense power but also a profound example of how obedience to God's will, even in the most challenging and seemingly impossible situations, can bring about miraculous and wondrous outcomes. The parting of the Red Sea is a reminder that when we are willing to follow God's directions, even when those directions seem difficult, confusing, or risky, we open ourselves up to experiencing God's wonders in ways that far exceed our expectations. Moses' willingness to obey God's command to stretch out his hand over the sea was an act of faith, one that led to the deliverance of the entire nation of Israel from the clutches of the Egyptians. This teaches us that obedience to God, especially in hard times, is not only about following rules but about trusting God's wisdom, power, and timing. When we obey, we invite God to work mightily in our lives, turning what appears to be a dead end into a pathway of victory and deliverance.

Obedience is often challenging, especially when we find ourselves in situations where the outcome is uncertain or when following God's instructions seems to go against our instincts or logic. For Moses and the Israelites, standing on the shores of the Red Sea with the Egyptian army fast approaching, the situation seemed hopeless. They were trapped, with nowhere to go and no apparent way of escape. From a human perspective, it might have seemed more logical to prepare for battle or to try to negotiate with the Egyptians rather than waiting for something miraculous to happen. But God's command to Moses was clear: stretch out your hand over the sea. In that moment, Moses had a choice—he could have given in to fear and doubt, or he could obey God, even though the command seemed strange and the outcome was unknown. Moses chose to obey, and that simple act of obedience led to one of the greatest miracles recorded in Scripture. The Red Sea parted, and the Israelites were able to walk through on dry ground. This teaches us that obedience to God, even when it seems difficult or when we don't fully understand His plan, positions us to experience His miraculous intervention in our lives.

The parting of the Red Sea was not only a demonstration of God's power over nature but also a testament to His faithfulness in fulfilling His promises. God had promised to deliver the Israelites from Egypt, and although the path to freedom led them through a seemingly impossible situation, God was faithful to His word. Moses' willingness to obey God's instructions, even when the situation seemed dire, was key to unlocking the fulfillment of that promise. This teaches us that when we are obedient to God's will, we become participants in the fulfillment of His promises for our lives. Obedience is often the bridge between God's promises and their realization. It is through our willingness to follow His lead, even when we don't see the full picture, that we align ourselves with His plans and purposes. Just as Moses' obedience led to the Israelites' deliverance, our obedience to God can lead to breakthroughs, blessings, and wonders that we could never achieve on our own.

Moreover, Moses' obedience in this moment serves as an example of what it means to trust God fully. Stretching out his hand over the sea was not a small or insignificant act—it was a bold declaration of faith in God's ability to do the impossible. Moses had no power in himself to part the sea; the miracle came entirely from God. But Moses' willingness to obey was the catalyst that set God's plan into motion. This teaches us that obedience is often an act of faith, a way of saying, "God, I trust You enough to follow Your instructions, even though I don't know how everything will turn out." When we step out in faith and obey God, we demonstrate our trust in His power and His goodness. We acknowledge that He is in control and that He knows what is best, even when we don't understand how things will work out. Moses' obedience to God's command teaches us that faith and obedience are inseparable. True faith is not just about believing in God's power; it's about acting on that belief, even when the way forward seems unclear.

The Israelites, too, had to obey God's instructions in this moment. After the sea was parted, they were commanded to walk through the waters on dry ground. This was no easy task. Imagine the fear and uncertainty they must have felt as they stepped into the seabed, with walls of water towering on either side. It would have been easy to hesitate or to doubt whether the waters would stay parted long enough for them to make it across. But just as Moses obeyed God's command to stretch out his hand, the Israelites had to obey the command to walk forward. This teaches us that obedience is not just for leaders like Moses; it is for all of God's people. Each of us is called to obey God's instructions, even when doing so requires us to step into situations that feel uncertain or risky. Just as the Israelites had to trust that God would hold back the waters, we must trust that God will protect us and provide for us as we walk in obedience to His will.

One of the most powerful aspects of this story is that obedience to God often leads to not only personal deliverance but also to the deliverance of others. Moses' willingness to obey God's command to part the sea didn't just benefit him—it resulted in the salvation of the entire Israelite nation. This teaches us that our obedience to God has a ripple effect. When we choose to follow God's will, we become vessels through which He can work in the lives of others. Our obedience can open doors for others to experience God's grace, deliverance, and blessing. Just as Moses' obedience led the Israelites to freedom, our obedience can lead others to experience the wonders of God's love and power in their own lives. This reminds us that our obedience is not just about us—it's about being part of God's larger plan to bring His kingdom to earth and to bless those around us.

Obedience to God often requires us to move forward in the face of fear and uncertainty. The Israelites were standing before the Red Sea, with the Egyptian army bearing down on them, and from a human perspective, the situation seemed hopeless. But God's instructions were clear: move forward. In the same way, God often calls us to step out in faith and obedience, even when we are afraid or unsure of the outcome. Obedience doesn't mean we won't feel fear; it means that we choose to follow God's instructions despite our fear. When we are willing to obey, even when it's hard, God meets us in that place of faith and works wonders on our behalf. The parting of the Red Sea shows us that God is able to do the impossible, but our role is to be willing to obey, to take that first step of faith, and to trust that God will do the rest.

The wonder of the Red Sea miracle also teaches us that obedience leads to a greater revelation of God's power and glory. When Moses obeyed God's command to stretch out his hand over the sea, the Israelites witnessed firsthand the power of God to control nature and to deliver His people in miraculous ways. This experience deepened their understanding of who God is and strengthened their faith in His ability to protect and provide for them.

Similarly, when we choose to obey God, we open ourselves up to experiencing more of His power and glory in our own lives. Obedience is the key to unlocking a deeper relationship with God, one in which we see His hand at work in ways we never thought possible. When we obey, we are positioned to witness God's wonders and to grow in our faith and trust in Him.

The parting of the Red Sea also illustrates that obedience requires persistence. The Bible tells us that the wind blew all night, parting the waters and drying the ground. This wasn't an instant miracle—it was a process that took time. Moses and the Israelites had to remain obedient and patient as they waited for the way to be fully prepared. This teaches us that obedience often involves waiting and persistence. Sometimes, we don't see the results of our obedience right away, but that doesn't mean God isn't working. Just as the Israelites had to wait for the sea to part completely, we must be willing to continue obeying God's instructions, even when the results aren't immediate. Persistence in obedience is key to experiencing the full wonder of God's plans for our lives.

In Exodus 14:26-27, after the Israelites had crossed the Red Sea, God instructed Moses to stretch out his hand over the sea again, and the waters returned, covering the Egyptian army and ensuring the Israelites' safety. This teaches us that obedience to God doesn't just lead to deliverance; it leads to complete victory. God's plan was not only to deliver the Israelites but also to destroy their enemies and remove the threat once and for all. When we obey God, He doesn't just bring us through difficult situations—He gives us victory over the challenges and obstacles we face. The same sea that had seemed like an obstacle became the very thing God used to defeat the Egyptians. This teaches us that God can use the very things that seem to be against us to bring about our victory when we obey His instructions.

In conclusion, Exodus 14:21-22, 26-27 teaches us the profound truth that willingness to obey brings wonders. When Moses obeyed God's command to stretch out his hand over the sea, a miraculous deliverance took place. The Red Sea parted, and the Israelites walked through on dry ground, escaping their enemies and witnessing the power of God in a way they had never seen before. This story reminds us that obedience to God's will, even in hard times, is the key to experiencing His miraculous intervention in our lives. Obedience is an act of faith, trust, and surrender, and it positions us to receive the fullness of

God's promises and blessings. Just as Moses' obedience led to the deliverance of the Israelites, our obedience can lead to breakthroughs, victories, and wonders that we could never achieve on our own. God calls us to be willing to obey, even when it's difficult, even when we don't understand, and even when we're afraid. When we choose to obey, we open the door for God to work mightily in our lives, turning impossible situations into pathways of victory and revealing His power and glory in ways that exceed our wildest expectations. Obedience to God brings wonders, and through it, we experience the fullness of His love, grace, and provision.

Chapter 5 - Walk Through the Waters

In Exodus 14:21-22, 26-27, we are given one of the most remarkable examples of God's power and faithfulness. The Israelites found themselves in an impossible situation, trapped between the Red Sea on one side and the approaching Egyptian army on the other. To their eyes, there was no escape. The sea was an insurmountable barrier, and the Egyptians, with their chariots and soldiers, were drawing closer by the moment. Fear gripped the hearts of the Israelites as they questioned their decision to leave Egypt and cried out to Moses, wondering if they were about to meet their demise in the wilderness. But what they couldn't see in that moment of fear and doubt was that God had a plan, a plan that would demonstrate His mighty power and faithful provision in a way they had never experienced before. In response to their fear, Moses declared, "Fear ye not, stand still, and see the salvation of the Lord" (Exodus 14:13), and then God instructed Moses to stretch out his hand over the sea. What happened next was nothing short of miraculous. God sent a powerful wind that parted the waters of the Red Sea, creating a dry path for the Israelites to walk through. This was more than just a moment of deliverance; it was a profound demonstration of how God can create a way through even the most insurmountable difficulties. What seemed like an impossible wall of water became a walkway of deliverance when God intervened. This powerful act reminds us that when we face challenges that seem overwhelming, God is able to guide us through the waters, turning barriers into pathways and impossibilities into opportunities for His glory.

Walking through the waters of the Red Sea required an incredible act of faith from the Israelites. The sea had been a symbol of fear and danger, something that they could not cross on their own. But when God parted the waters, He transformed that very obstacle into a path of deliverance. The waters that had once represented certain death now stood as walls on either side, held back by the power of God, while the dry ground beneath their feet became the way to their freedom. This teaches us a profound lesson about faith and trust. Often in life, we find ourselves facing situations that seem just as daunting as the Red Sea—challenges that appear to have no solution, problems that seem too big to overcome. In those moments, it's easy to feel trapped, just as the Israelites did. But God is always at work, and just as He parted the Red Sea, He can part the waters in our lives, making a way where there seems to be no way. The key is to have the faith to step forward, to walk through the waters, trusting that God will hold them back and guide us safely to the other side. Just as the Israelites had to walk through the waters in faith, we, too, are called to walk in faith, believing that God will guide us through whatever difficulties we face.

This act of walking through the waters also represents the journey of faith itself. God doesn't always remove the obstacles from our lives completely; instead, He often provides a way through them. The Israelites still had to walk through the sea—they had to step into the unknown, with the waters towering above them on both sides. It wasn't an easy or comfortable journey, but it was the path God had created for their deliverance. In the same way, we often have to walk through difficult circumstances, trusting that God will guide us safely through. The path may not always be easy, and the waters may seem overwhelming, but God promises to be with us every step of the way. The story of the Red Sea reminds us that God doesn't abandon us in our struggles. He doesn't leave us to figure things out on our own. Instead, He goes before us, creating a path through the challenges, and walks with us as we journey through them. What seems like an insurmountable obstacle becomes a walkway of faith when God is involved.

Moreover, walking through the waters teaches us about the transformative power of obedience. When God instructed Moses to stretch out his hand over the sea, Moses obeyed, even though the command must have seemed strange and the situation seemed impossible. His obedience set the stage for the miracle to unfold. Similarly, the Israelites had to obey God's command to walk through the waters, trusting that He would keep the waters held back until they reached the other side. This teaches us that when we are obedient to God's commands, even in the face of uncertainty or fear, we open the door for God to work in miraculous ways. Obedience is often the first step in experiencing God's provision and deliverance. When we choose to walk in the path that God has laid out for us, even when it's difficult or frightening, we demonstrate our trust in His plan and His power. The Israelites' willingness to walk through the waters of the Red Sea is a powerful example of how obedience to God leads to deliverance and victory. It reminds us that even when the way forward seems uncertain, we can trust that God's path is the best path, and that He will guide us safely through whatever challenges we face.

The imagery of walking through the waters also reminds us that God is in control of the elements, of the circumstances, and of every aspect of our lives. The Red Sea, which had seemed like an unconquerable barrier, was under God's command. He controlled the wind and the waves, and He held the waters back until His people were safely across. This demonstrates God's absolute authority over nature and over every obstacle we face. When we feel overwhelmed by the "waters" of life—the difficulties, fears, and uncertainties that threaten to overtake us—we can take comfort in the fact that God is sovereign. He has the power to part the waters, to make a way where there is no way, and to protect us as we walk through. The story of the Red Sea is a reminder that nothing is too difficult for God. What seems impossible to us is entirely possible with Him. He is the one who can turn a sea into a highway, transforming our greatest challenges into opportunities for deliverance and growth. Walking through the waters means trusting in God's sovereignty and believing that He has the power to guide us through even the most difficult situations.

As we reflect on the Israelites' journey through the Red Sea, it's also important to recognize that walking through the waters was not just about physical deliverance—it was about spiritual transformation. The Red Sea marked the transition from slavery to freedom for the Israelites. They had been in bondage in Egypt for generations, but now they were on the path to becoming God's chosen people, free to serve and worship Him. Walking through the waters represented a new beginning for them, a step into their identity as God's people. In the same way, the challenges we face in life are often opportunities for spiritual growth and transformation. As we walk through the "waters" of difficulty, God is not only delivering us from our immediate problems—He is shaping us, refining us, and drawing us closer to Himself. The Red Sea experience was a turning point for the Israelites, and it can be a turning point for us as well. When we trust God to guide us through our challenges, we emerge on the other side not only delivered but also transformed, with a deeper faith and a stronger relationship with Him.

Another important lesson we learn from walking through the waters is that God's deliverance is complete. In Exodus 14:26-27, after the Israelites had safely crossed the sea, God commanded Moses to stretch out his hand again, and the waters returned, covering the Egyptian army and destroying them. The same waters that had been a path of deliverance for the Israelites became a means of judgment for their enemies. This teaches us that when God delivers us, He does so completely. He not only brings us through our difficulties, but He also deals with the things that threaten to destroy us. The Egyptians, who had pursued the Israelites with the intent to capture or kill them, were completely defeated by God's intervention. In the same way, when we trust God to guide us through the waters, we can be confident that He will not only bring us to safety but also defeat the forces that seek to harm us. God's deliverance is thorough and final. He is not content to simply bring us through our challenges—He also ensures that the things that once threatened us are dealt with, so that we can move forward in freedom and peace.

Walking through the waters of the Red Sea also teaches us about the power of community and the importance of walking together in faith. The Israelites didn't cross the sea individually—they walked through the waters as a community, united in their trust in God and their desire for freedom. This reminds us that we are not meant to walk through the waters of life alone. God has placed us in communities—families, churches, and friendships—so that we can support and encourage one another as we journey through life's challenges. Just as the Israelites walked together through the sea, we are called to walk alongside one another, bearing each other's burdens and reminding each other of God's faithfulness. Walking through the waters together strengthens our faith and deepens our sense of connection to God and to one another. The Red Sea experience was not just a personal journey for each Israelite—it was a collective experience that shaped them as a people. In the same way, our shared experiences of walking through the waters of difficulty can strengthen the bonds of community and draw us closer to God.

In conclusion, Exodus 14:21-22, 26-27 provides a powerful and compelling lesson about walking through the waters. God created a path through the Red Sea, transforming what seemed like an impossible barrier into a walkway of deliverance for the Israelites. This story teaches us that no matter how daunting our challenges may seem, God is able to guide us through them. He is the one who can part the waters in our lives, making a way where there seems to be no way. Walking through the waters requires faith, trust, and obedience. It means stepping forward even when the path ahead seems uncertain, trusting that God will hold back the waters and guide us safely to the other side. It also means recognizing that God is in control of every aspect of our lives, and that He has the power to turn our greatest obstacles into opportunities for deliverance and transformation. Just as the Israelites walked through the waters of the Red Sea, we are called to walk through the challenges of life with faith and trust in God's provision. And as we do, we can be confident that God's deliverance is complete, His power is sufficient, and His love is unfailing. The story of the Red Sea reminds us that when we walk through the waters with God, what once seemed impossible becomes possible, and what once seemed like a barrier becomes a pathway to freedom, growth, and victory.

Chapter 6 - Witness to God's Presence

In Exodus 14:21-22, 26-27, we are given a breathtaking display of God's presence and power as He leads the Israelites through one of the most harrowing and miraculous moments in their history—the parting of the Red Sea. This story isn't just about God's ability to manipulate the forces of nature; it's about His constant presence with His people, guiding and protecting them in ways that made His presence undeniable. The Israelites, having just escaped the horrors of slavery in Egypt, found themselves trapped between the advancing Egyptian army and the Red Sea, a seemingly impossible situation. Fear and panic swept through the camp as the people cried out, not knowing how they would escape this deadly predicament. But throughout their journey, God made His presence known to them in a visible, tangible way—through a pillar of cloud by day and a pillar of fire by night. These pillars were more than just guiding lights; they were powerful reminders of God's presence with His people. To witness God's presence in such a direct way must have been both awe-inspiring and comforting. It's one thing to believe that God is with you in theory, but it's another to see it manifest before your eyes in such a dramatic and undeniable form. These pillars became symbols of God's unyielding guidance, protection, and faithfulness, and they showed the Israelites that no matter how impossible their circumstances seemed, they were never alone. Witnessing God's presence firsthand brings strength and security through even the most terrifying storms of life, and this lesson resonates deeply with us today, reminding us that God is with us always, even when we can't see a literal pillar of cloud or fire in front of us.

The presence of the pillar of cloud by day and the pillar of fire by night was more than just a navigational aid for the Israelites. These visible signs of God's presence carried a profound spiritual significance. As the Israelites journeyed through the wilderness, these pillars served as constant reminders that God was leading them, even when the path seemed uncertain. When the Egyptian army was bearing down on them, the pillars represented God's unwavering commitment to His people's safety. As Exodus 14:19 tells us, "And the angel of God, which went before the camp of Israel, removed and went behind them; and the pillar of the cloud went from before their face, and stood behind them."

This divine repositioning of the pillar was a powerful demonstration of God's protective presence. Not only was God leading them forward, but He also placed Himself between the Israelites and their enemies, shielding them from the approaching danger. The pillar of cloud, now acting as a barrier between the Israelites and the Egyptians, showed that God was not only guiding them but actively protecting them from harm. This teaches us that God's presence is not passive; it's active and intentional. He doesn't just walk ahead of us, showing us the way—He also stands between us and the forces that seek to destroy us, providing a shield of protection that no earthly force can penetrate.

As the Israelites stood at the edge of the Red Sea, trapped between the waters and the Egyptian army, the pillar of cloud gave them the reassurance they needed in that moment of fear. It must have been terrifying to see the enemy closing in with no clear escape, yet the sight of God's presence in the pillar gave them the strength to hold on, even when everything seemed hopeless. This is a powerful reminder that witnessing God's presence in our lives can give us the courage to face seemingly insurmountable challenges. Just as the pillar of cloud stood between the Israelites and the Egyptians, God's presence stands between us and the fears, doubts, and dangers that threaten to overwhelm us. When we witness God's presence in our lives—whether through answered prayers, moments of peace in chaos, or His guidance in uncertain times—we are reminded that He is with us, shielding us and fighting on our behalf. The Israelites were about to experience one of the most miraculous events in their history, but before that happened, they had to trust in the visible sign of God's presence. The same is true for us today. Before we see God's full deliverance in our own lives, we must first trust in His presence, knowing that He is with us every step of the way, even when the path ahead seems impossible.

The pillar of cloud by day and the pillar of fire by night also symbolize the dual nature of God's presence: guidance and protection. By day, the Israelites followed the cloud, knowing that it represented God's direction for their journey. They didn't have to worry about finding the right path because the cloud led them exactly where they needed to go. By night, the pillar of fire illuminated the darkness, providing both light and warmth in the cold desert night. This fire was a tangible expression of God's care for His people, showing them that He would be with them, even in the darkest and most challenging moments. For the Israelites, this was more than just a practical form of guidance—it was a constant reminder that they were never alone. God was with them in the light of day and in the darkness of night. This dual presence reminds us that God is with us in every season of life, in the bright and easy days as well as the dark and difficult nights. Whether we are walking through the daylight of success and joy or navigating the night of trial and fear, God's presence is always with us, guiding and protecting us, just as He did for the Israelites.

When Moses stretched out his hand over the Red Sea, and the waters parted, it was not just an act of power, but a continuation of God's visible presence with His people. The Israelites had witnessed God's presence in the pillars, and now they were about to witness His presence in an even more dramatic way—as the sea itself obeyed His command and opened up a path for them to walk through. Exodus 14:21-22 describes this incredible moment: "And Moses stretched out his hand over the sea; and the Lord caused the sea to go back by a strong east wind all that night, and made the sea dry land, and the waters were divided. And the children of Israel went into the midst of the sea upon the dry ground: and the waters were a wall unto them on their right hand, and on their left." The parting of the Red Sea was a visible and undeniable confirmation of God's presence with His people. The walls of water on either side of them as they walked through the sea were like a shield, protecting them from the forces of nature and from the Egyptian army that pursued them. This miraculous event showed the Israelites that God's presence was not limited to the pillars of cloud and fire—He was with them in the very elements of nature, commanding the wind and the sea to do His bidding. This teaches us that God's presence is not confined to specific places or forms; He is present in every aspect of our lives, working in ways we may not always see or understand but that are always for our good and His glory.

Witnessing God's presence in such a powerful and direct way must have strengthened the Israelites' faith and trust in Him. As they walked through the Red Sea, with the waters held back by God's command, they were walking through a miracle. Each step they took on the dry ground was a testament to God's power and faithfulness. It's one thing to hear about God's presence or to believe in it on a theoretical level, but it's another thing entirely to witness it in such a tangible and undeniable way. The Israelites had seen the plagues in Egypt, they had witnessed God's protection during the Passover, and now they were walking through the very waters that had once seemed like an impassable barrier. This experience would become a foundational memory for the Israelites, a moment they would look back on time and time again as proof of God's faithfulness and presence with them. In our own lives, we may not witness the parting of a sea, but we can experience God's presence in profound ways that strengthen our faith and give us the courage to keep moving forward. When we witness God's presence—whether through answered prayers, unexpected blessings, or moments of peace in the midst of chaos—it reminds us that He is with us, guiding us, protecting us, and leading us through the storms of life.

Exodus 14:26-27 continues the story, showing us that God's presence not only led the Israelites through the sea but also brought about their complete deliverance from the Egyptians. After the Israelites had crossed safely to the other side, God instructed Moses to stretch out his hand again, and the waters returned to their place, covering the Egyptians and their chariots. "And the waters returned, and covered the chariots, and the horsemen, and all the host of Pharaoh that came into the sea after them; there remained not so much as one of them." The same waters that had been a path of deliverance for the Israelites became a means of judgment for the Egyptians. This teaches us that God's presence is not only a source of guidance and protection for His people but also a force of justice and righteousness. The Egyptians had sought to enslave and destroy the Israelites, but God's presence intervened on behalf of His people, ensuring that their enemies would not prevail. This is a powerful reminder that God's presence brings not only comfort and peace but also justice and deliverance. When we witness God's presence in our lives, we can trust that He is not only guiding us but also working on our behalf to bring about justice and to protect us from those who seek to harm us.

The pillars of cloud and fire, along with the parting of the Red Sea, serve as a powerful witness to God's faithfulness. They show us that God is not distant or removed from the struggles of His people—He is present, involved, and actively working on our behalf. For the Israelites, these visible signs of God's presence were a source of strength and security, reminding them that no matter how difficult or dangerous their journey became, they were never alone. This is a lesson that resonates deeply with us today. In our own lives, we may not see a literal pillar of cloud or fire, but we can witness God's presence in countless ways. Through His Word, through the peace that comes from prayer, through the support of fellow believers, and through the many ways He provides and cares for us, we can experience His presence in our daily lives. And just as the Israelites found strength and security in the visible signs of God's presence, we too can find peace and confidence in knowing that God is always with us, guiding us, protecting us, and leading us through the storms and challenges we face.

In conclusion, Exodus 14:21-22, 26-27 reminds us of the incredible power of witnessing God's presence. The pillars of cloud and fire were visible signs that God was with His people, leading them through the wilderness and protecting them from their enemies. The parting of the Red Sea was a dramatic confirmation of God's presence, showing that He is not only a guide but also a deliverer, able to turn even the most impossible situations into pathways of freedom and victory. As the Israelites walked through the sea on dry ground, they were walking through a miracle, a tangible expression of God's power and faithfulness. This experience strengthened their faith and gave them the courage to continue on their journey, knowing that God was with them every step of the way. For us today, the story of the Red Sea serves as a powerful reminder that God's presence is with us in every moment of our lives. Whether we are facing challenges, dangers, or uncertainties, we can trust that God is there, guiding us, protecting us, and leading us through to the other side. Witnessing God's presence in our lives brings strength, peace, and security, reminding us that we are never alone, and that with God by our side, we can face any storm with confidence and faith.

Chapter 7 - Wipe Out the Enemy Completely

In Exodus 14:21-22, 26-27, we witness one of the most dramatic and powerful displays of God's intervention in the lives of His people. The Israelites, having just escaped slavery in Egypt, found themselves in a seemingly impossible situation: trapped between the vast, impassable Red Sea and the mighty Egyptian army that had pursued them. The Egyptians, equipped with chariots and armed to the teeth, were bearing down on the Israelites, who had no weapons and no military training. They were in a desperate situation, and fear and panic swept through their ranks. But what the Israelites didn't realize at that moment was that God had not only brought them to this place of danger to deliver them, but He also had a plan to wipe out their enemies completely. This story is not just about God's power to protect, but about His ability to completely eradicate the threats His people face. When the Egyptians followed the Israelites into the path God had created through the Red Sea, God closed the waters over them, wiping them out entirely. "And the waters returned, and covered the chariots, and the horsemen, and all the host of Pharaoh that came into the sea after them; there remained not so much as one of them" (Exodus 14:28). The same waters that had parted to deliver the Israelites became the instrument of judgment for the Egyptians. This teaches us that God doesn't just protect us from danger—He removes the danger entirely. He wipes out the threats we face completely, ensuring that they no longer have power over us. The destruction of the Egyptian army was not just a moment of deliverance; it was a decisive victory that guaranteed the Israelites' freedom and safety moving forward.

The complete eradication of the Egyptian army is a profound example of how God deals with the enemies of His people. The Egyptians were relentless in their pursuit of the Israelites, refusing to give up even after the ten plagues and the death of their firstborn sons. Pharaoh's heart had been hardened, and he was determined to bring the Israelites back into bondage. But God had other plans. He wasn't just going to allow the Israelites to escape temporarily—He was going to ensure that the Egyptians would never again pose a threat to His people. By wiping out the Egyptian army completely, God was making a statement: the enemies of His people would not have the final word. This teaches us that when God steps in to deliver us, He doesn't leave the job half done. He finishes it completely, removing the enemy's power and influence over our lives. Just as the Egyptian army was utterly destroyed, so too can the things that threaten us be wiped out by God's intervention.

The image of the waters of the Red Sea crashing down upon the Egyptians is a vivid reminder of God's justice and power. Throughout the story of the Exodus, we see how Pharaoh and the Egyptians had oppressed the Israelites for generations, subjecting them to cruel and inhumane treatment. They had enslaved God's people, working them ruthlessly and trying to break their spirits. The Israelites had cried out to God for deliverance, and God had heard their cries. The ten plagues that struck Egypt were a form of divine judgment, but Pharaoh's heart remained hardened. Even after the Israelites left Egypt, Pharaoh couldn't let go of his desire to control and dominate them, so he pursued them to the edge of the Red Sea. But God, in His righteousness, brought swift and final judgment upon Pharaoh and his army. The complete destruction of the Egyptian forces was God's way of saying that injustice would not prevail, and that He would defend His people to the very end. This teaches us that God's justice is not only swift but also complete. He doesn't just deliver His people from oppression—He destroys the oppressor.

In our own lives, we often face enemies and threats that seem overwhelming. These enemies may not take the form of literal armies, but they can be just as dangerous. We may face enemies like fear, doubt, addiction, sin, or even people who seek to harm us or hinder our progress. These threats can seem insurmountable, just as the Egyptian army must have seemed to the Israelites. But the story of the Red Sea reminds us that God is not only capable of protecting us from these threats—He can wipe them out completely. When God intervenes on our behalf, He doesn't just offer temporary relief from our problems. He offers total and complete deliverance. Just as the waters of the Red Sea wiped out the Egyptians, God can completely destroy the forces that seek to harm us. This teaches us that God's deliverance is thorough and final. When He steps in, He leaves no trace of the enemy behind. The things that once threatened to overwhelm us are swept away by His power.

The complete destruction of the Egyptian army also serves as a powerful symbol of God's sovereignty. The Egyptians were a formidable military power, and Pharaoh was one of the most powerful rulers in the world at the time. From a human perspective, the Israelites stood no chance against such a force. They were outnumbered, outgunned, and untrained for battle. But God's power is not limited by human strength or weakness. He is the Creator of the universe, and all things are subject to His will. When God decided to wipe out the Egyptian army, there was nothing Pharaoh or his soldiers could do to stop it. The waters of the Red Sea, which had been held back by God's command, were released at the exact moment He chose, and the Egyptian forces were completely wiped out. This teaches us that no enemy, no matter how powerful or intimidating, can stand against the will of God. When God decides to act, nothing can stop Him. His power is absolute, and His victory is assured.

Another important aspect of this story is that the destruction of the Egyptian army was not just about physical deliverance—it was also about spiritual freedom. The Israelites had been in bondage for so long that their identity as God's chosen people had been overshadowed by their identity as slaves. They had been oppressed and dehumanized, and their sense of hope and purpose had been diminished. By wiping out the Egyptian army, God was not only freeing them from physical slavery but also restoring their sense of dignity and worth. The complete destruction of their enemies was a sign that their past was truly behind them, and that they were now free to step into the future that God had prepared for them. This teaches us that when God wipes out the enemies in our lives, He is also restoring our identity and our sense of purpose. He is reminding us that we are His children, and that nothing can separate us from His love and protection.

The destruction of the Egyptians also serves as a warning to those who oppose God and His people. Pharaoh and his army were determined to defy God's will and to continue oppressing the Israelites, even after witnessing the power of God through the ten plagues. They thought they could pursue God's people and bring them back into bondage, but they were wrong. God's judgment upon them was swift and final. This teaches us that those who stand against God's people ultimately stand against God Himself, and no one can oppose God and win. The destruction of the Egyptian army is a reminder that God's justice will prevail, and that those who seek to harm His people will face His judgment. It is also a reminder to us that we need not fear those who oppose us, because God is our defender and protector. Just as He wiped out the Egyptian army, He will wipe out the forces that seek to harm us.

The story of the Red Sea also teaches us that God's timing is perfect. The waters did not crash down on the Egyptians by accident—they did so at the exact moment that God had ordained. God waited until the Israelites were safely on the other side before He released the waters to destroy the Egyptians. This teaches us that God's deliverance is not only complete but also perfectly timed. He knows exactly when to act, and He ensures that His people are safe before He brings judgment upon their enemies. This is a comforting reminder that God is always in control, even when the situation seems dire. The Israelites may have felt trapped and afraid as the Egyptians pursued them, but God knew exactly what He was doing. He had a plan to deliver them and to wipe out their enemies at the right moment. This teaches us to trust in God's timing, even when we feel overwhelmed or afraid. God is always working behind the scenes, and when the time is right, He will act decisively on our behalf.

In conclusion, Exodus 14:21-22, 26-27 teaches us a profound lesson about God's ability to wipe out the enemies we face completely. The destruction of the Egyptian army was not just a moment of physical deliverance for the Israelites—it was a demonstration of God's power, justice, and faithfulness. It showed that God doesn't just protect His people from danger—He removes the danger entirely, ensuring that it no longer has power over them. The waters of the Red Sea, which had once seemed like an insurmountable obstacle, became the instrument of God's judgment, wiping out the enemies of His people completely. This story teaches us that when we face enemies in our own lives, whether they are physical, emotional, or spiritual, we can trust that God is able to wipe them out completely. He doesn't just offer temporary relief—He offers total and complete deliverance. Just as the Egyptian army was destroyed, so too can the forces that seek to harm us be wiped out by God's power. We can trust in His sovereignty, His timing, and His ability to bring about complete victory in our lives. When God intervenes, He finishes the job entirely, leaving no trace of the enemy behind. The story of the Red Sea reminds us that with God on our side, we have nothing to fear, because He will wipe out the enemies we face completely, securing our freedom and safety for the future.

Chapter 8 - Wait and Witness God's Salvation

In Exodus 14:21-22, 26-27, we witness one of the most astonishing moments in the Bible: the parting of the Red Sea, a story filled with awe, fear, and ultimately, salvation. The Israelites, having just escaped from centuries of slavery in Egypt, were on a perilous journey to freedom when they found themselves trapped between the vast waters of the Red Sea and the approaching Egyptian army. It must have felt like a hopeless situation to them, with no way to move forward and no way to retreat. Panic set in as they saw the Egyptians closing in, chariots thundering toward them. They cried out in fear, wondering why they had been led to this impossible place. But in that moment of terror, Moses spoke words of faith that would change everything. He told the people to wait and witness the salvation of the Lord: "Fear ye not, stand still, and see the salvation of the Lord, which he will show to you today: for the Egyptians whom ye have seen today, ye shall see them again no more forever" (Exodus 14:13). This was a command to stop, to wait, and to trust that God would act on their behalf. Sometimes in life, when we face seemingly impossible situations, the hardest thing to do is to wait. Our natural instinct is to panic, to try to find our own solutions, or to give up in despair. But the story of the Red Sea teaches us that there are moments when we must be still, stop trying to fix things on our own, and wait to witness God's salvation unfold. It's in those moments of waiting that God often does His most miraculous work.

The idea of waiting on God's salvation is challenging for most of us because waiting requires patience, trust, and faith—three things that don't come easily when we are surrounded by fear or uncertainty. The Israelites were faced with what seemed like an insurmountable obstacle: the waters of the Red Sea on one side and an enemy determined to destroy them on the other. From a human perspective, there was no solution, no way out. But Moses reminded them that their salvation wasn't something they could achieve on their own; it was something God would provide. He told them to "stand still." This is perhaps one of the hardest commands to obey when we are faced with trouble. When our backs are against the wall, we want to act, to do something, anything, to try to change our circumstances. But Moses' words remind us that sometimes the best thing we can do is to stop, to be still, and to wait for God to act. This teaches us an important lesson about faith: faith isn't just about doing; it's also about trusting in God's timing and allowing Him to work on our behalf in His own way.

In this story, we see that waiting on God doesn't mean doing nothing; rather, it means trusting that God is already working, even if we can't see it yet. The Israelites couldn't see the wind that God sent to part the Red Sea at first, but that didn't mean it wasn't happening. The Bible tells us that "the Lord caused the sea to go back by a strong east wind all that night, and made the sea dry land, and the waters were divided" (Exodus 14:21). While the Israelites were waiting, God was working, sending a wind that would make the impossible possible. The same is true in our own lives. When we are called to wait on God's salvation, we can trust that He is at work behind the scenes, orchestrating things in ways we may not understand. It may take time, and it may not happen in the way we expect, but God is always working on behalf of His people. The wind that God sent to part the Red Sea didn't act instantly; it blew all night, slowly but surely pushing the waters back until there was dry land for the Israelites to walk on. This teaches us that sometimes God's work takes time. The miracle may not happen in a moment, but it will happen in His perfect timing.

Waiting on God requires us to surrender our desire for control. The Israelites were powerless to change their situation, and the same is often true for us. When we face difficulties—whether they are financial struggles, health crises, broken relationships, or personal failures—it's easy to feel like we need to take control and fix things ourselves. But the story of the Red Sea reminds us that there are times when we need to step back and let God take control. The Israelites had no way of parting the sea on their own, and they had no way of defeating the Egyptian army. Their only option was to trust in God's power and to wait for His salvation. This teaches us that sometimes, the greatest act of faith is letting go of our need to control the situation and trusting that God will make a way where there seems to be no way. When we surrender control to God, we open ourselves up to witnessing His power in ways we could never have imagined.

The parting of the Red Sea is one of the most dramatic examples in Scripture of God's power to save, and it shows us that God's salvation often comes in ways we don't expect. The Israelites were expecting a battle with the

Egyptians, but God had a different plan. He didn't just deliver them from their enemies—He wiped the enemy out completely, ensuring that they would never have to face them again. When Moses stretched out his hand over the sea, and the waters returned to their place, the Egyptian army was swallowed up, and not one of them survived: "And the waters returned, and covered the chariots, and the horsemen, and all the host of Pharaoh that came into the sea after them; there remained not so much as one of them" (Exodus 14:28). This teaches us that God's salvation is thorough and complete. When He delivers us, He doesn't leave the job half-done. He finishes what He starts. The Israelites were not only saved from immediate danger, but they were also delivered from the threat of the Egyptians once and for all. This reminds us that when we wait on God's salvation, we can trust that His deliverance will be full and final.

Another key lesson from the parting of the Red Sea is that waiting on God allows us to witness His glory in ways we might otherwise miss. If the Israelites had tried to fight the Egyptians on their own or had panicked and tried to flee, they would never have experienced the miraculous power of God in parting the sea. By waiting and trusting in God's salvation, they were able to witness one of the most incredible miracles in history. This teaches us that when we wait on God, we position ourselves to witness His glory and His power at work in our lives. We may not always understand why we are being asked to wait, and the waiting may be difficult, but when we do, we often see God's hand in ways that far exceed our expectations. The Israelites not only witnessed God's power in parting the sea, but they also saw His faithfulness in fulfilling His promises to deliver them from Egypt. Waiting on God allows us to witness His faithfulness and to see the ways in which He works all things together for our good.

The parting of the Red Sea also teaches us that waiting on God's salvation builds our faith. The Israelites had already seen God's power in the plagues that He sent upon Egypt, but the parting of the Red Sea took their faith to a whole new level. As they walked through the sea on dry ground, with walls of water towering on either side, they were walking through a miracle. Each step they took was an act of faith, trusting that the waters would remain parted until they had safely crossed. This experience would become a foundational memory for the Israelites, a moment they could look back on for the rest of their lives as proof of God's power and faithfulness. In the same way, when we wait on God's salvation and witness His work in our lives, our faith is strengthened. We are reminded that God is always with us, and that He is able to do far more than we could ever ask or imagine. Waiting on God gives us the opportunity to see His hand at work and to build a deeper, more trusting relationship with Him.

Waiting and witnessing God's salvation also teaches us about the importance of patience. The Israelites had to wait all night as the strong east wind blew and parted the waters. It didn't happen instantly, but it happened in God's perfect timing. This teaches us that God's work often requires patience. We live in a world that values instant gratification, but God's timing is often different from our own. The Israelites had to wait, but in the morning, they saw the results of God's work: a clear path through the sea that led to their deliverance. This reminds us that when we are asked to wait on God, it is not because He has forgotten us or because He is not working. It is because His timing is perfect, and sometimes the greatest miracles take time to unfold. Patience is a key part of the process of waiting on God's salvation, and when we learn to be patient, we open ourselves up to witnessing the full scope of His work in our lives.

The story of the Red Sea also shows us that waiting on God requires faith in His promises. God had promised to deliver the Israelites from Egypt, but the journey to that deliverance was not easy. They faced numerous challenges along the way, and the Red Sea was one of the greatest tests of their faith. But God's promises are always true, and He is always faithful to fulfill them. The Israelites had to trust in God's promise of deliverance, even when it seemed like they were facing an impossible situation. In the same way, we are called to trust in God's promises, even when our circumstances seem overwhelming. Waiting on God's salvation means trusting that He will fulfill His promises in His own time and in His own way. The parting of the Red Sea is a reminder that God is always faithful, and that His promises are never empty. When we wait on Him, we can trust that He will come through, just as He did for the Israelites.

Finally, the parting of the Red Sea teaches us that God's salvation is not just about rescuing us from danger—it's about leading us into freedom. The Israelites weren't just saved from the Egyptian army; they were led into a new life of freedom, a life where they would no longer be slaves but would be free to serve and worship God. This teaches us that when we wait on God's salvation, it's not just about being rescued from our immediate problems—it's about being led into a new life of purpose, joy, and freedom. God's salvation is transformative. It doesn't just change our circumstances; it changes us. The Israelites were no longer defined by their past as slaves; they were now God's chosen people, on their way to the Promised Land. In the same way, when we wait on God and witness His salvation in our lives, we are not just rescued from our problems—we are transformed, and we are led into a new life of freedom and purpose in Him.

In conclusion, Exodus 14:21-22, 26-27 teaches us the profound importance of waiting and witnessing God's salvation. Moses told the Israelites to stand still and see the salvation of the Lord, and in doing so, they witnessed one of the greatest miracles in history: the parting of the Red Sea. This story reminds us that there are times in life when we must stop, be still, and trust in God's power to save. Waiting on God requires patience, faith, and a willingness to let go of our need for control, but when we do, we open ourselves up to witnessing His miraculous work in our lives. Just as the Israelites were delivered from the Egyptians, we too can trust that God will deliver us from the challenges and difficulties we face. His salvation is complete, His timing is perfect, and His power is unmatched. When we wait on Him, we will witness His glory, His faithfulness, and His ability to make a way where there seems to be no way.

Chapter 9 - Weakness Turns to Worship

In Exodus 14:21-22, 26-27, we witness a transformation that reflects the journey of every believer: from weakness and fear to worship and faith. The Israelites, newly freed from centuries of slavery in Egypt, found themselves in a situation that seemed utterly hopeless. They were trapped between the vast, uncrossable Red Sea and the powerful Egyptian army that was fast approaching, led by Pharaoh, who had changed his mind about letting them go. For the Israelites, the Red Sea represented an insurmountable obstacle, and the sight of the Egyptian chariots barreling toward them filled them with fear and despair. They cried out in panic, questioning whether it had been better to remain in Egypt as slaves rather than die in the wilderness. They were weak, not just physically but also emotionally and spiritually. In that moment of weakness, it was easy to forget the mighty acts of God that had already delivered them from Pharaoh's grip through the ten plagues. Yet, this moment of desperation was the precursor to one of the greatest displays of God's power, and it is in this transition—from their weakness to their witness of God's deliverance—that we see a profound truth about the relationship between weakness and worship. In their moment of greatest vulnerability, God stepped in and transformed their weakness into a testimony of His might. When the Israelites saw the waters of the Red Sea miraculously part before their eyes and the dry land open up a path to safety, they experienced a dramatic shift. Their weakness, fear, and helplessness were replaced by awe, faith, and ultimately worship. This teaches us that our moments of greatest weakness can become the very moments that lead us to worship when we see God's hand at work in delivering us.

As the waters of the Red Sea stood up like walls on either side, the Israelites walked through the sea on dry ground. In Exodus 14:21-22, the text tells us, "And Moses stretched out his hand over the sea; and the Lord caused the sea to go back by a strong east wind all that night, and made the sea dry land, and the waters were divided. And the children of Israel went into the midst of the sea upon the dry ground: and the waters were a wall unto them on their right hand, and on their left." This was a moment of incredible power and grace from God. What had once seemed like an impassable barrier, a symbol of their powerlessness, became the very means of their salvation. It was as if God was saying, "What you see as an obstacle, I will turn into your deliverance." This is a lesson that speaks to all of us today. In the moments when we feel weak, when our circumstances seem impossible, God can take those very situations and turn them into opportunities to demonstrate His power. Our weakness is not the end of the story. Just as the Red Sea was not the end for the Israelites, but rather the beginning of their journey into freedom, our moments of weakness can be the very places where God works His greatest miracles.

The Israelites' weakness was further magnified by their lack of faith in that critical moment. As they saw the Egyptians advancing, their instinct was to doubt God's plan and His ability to save them. They complained to Moses, saying, "Because there were no graves in Egypt, hast thou taken us away to die in the wilderness?" (Exodus 14:11). This statement reflects the depth of their fear and their sense of abandonment. In their weakness, they could not see a way out. But this is exactly where God meets us—in the depths of our fear, doubt, and uncertainty. God didn't rebuke the Israelites for their lack of faith; instead, He used this moment to reveal His glory in an even more powerful way. This teaches us that God is not limited by our weakness or lack of faith. He understands our human frailty, and rather than abandoning us in our fear, He steps into our weakness with His strength. The Israelites' fear was met with God's reassurance and power as He parted the sea before them, showing them that His strength is made perfect in our weakness. This is a profound truth that carries through the entire Bible: God doesn't require us to be strong on our own; He asks us to trust Him in our weakness, and in doing so, we open the door for Him to act mightily on our behalf.

As the Israelites walked through the parted sea, their fear began to give way to awe. The walls of water towering on either side were a visible sign of God's presence and protection. They were walking through a miracle, and each step forward was a step further away from the fear that had once gripped them. In moments like these, when we witness God's deliverance firsthand, something shifts within us. Our perspective changes, and we move from a place of fear and weakness to a place of awe and gratitude. The Israelites' journey through the Red Sea was not just a physical journey; it was a spiritual one as well. With each step, they were moving from doubt to faith, from fear to trust, and from weakness to strength. This teaches us that when we are willing to step forward in faith, even in the midst of our weakness, we allow God to transform our situation. He takes what was meant for our destruction and turns it into a path of deliverance. The Red Sea, which had seemed like the end, became the means by which God led His people into a new beginning.

But the transformation from weakness to worship didn't stop when the Israelites reached the other side. In Exodus 14:26-27, we see the culmination of God's deliverance: "And the Lord said unto Moses, Stretch out thine hand over the sea, that the waters may come again upon the Egyptians, upon their chariots, and upon their horsemen. And Moses stretched forth his hand over the sea, and the sea returned to his strength when the morning appeared; and the Egyptians fled against it; and the Lord overthrew the Egyptians in the midst of the sea." The same waters that had provided a path of deliverance for the Israelites became the instrument of judgment for the Egyptians. God didn't just save His people; He wiped out the threat of their enemies entirely. This is a powerful reminder that when God delivers us, He does so completely. He doesn't leave us vulnerable to the same threats that once held us captive. Just as the Egyptians were swallowed up by the waters, the things that once threatened to destroy us are wiped out by God's intervention. This complete deliverance is what turns our weakness into worship. When we see not only that God has saved us, but that He has done so in a way that leaves no trace of our enemies, our response is one of awe and reverence. The Israelites, who had begun this journey in fear and weakness, now stood on the other side of the sea, witnessing the complete and total defeat of their enemies. Their response? Worship.

Exodus 15 records the song of worship that the Israelites sang in response to God's deliverance. "Then sang Moses and the children of Israel this song unto the Lord, and spake, saying, I will sing unto the Lord, for he hath triumphed gloriously: the horse and his rider hath he thrown into the sea" (Exodus 15:1). This song of worship was a direct response to what they had witnessed. They had seen God's hand at work, and it had transformed them from a people who were filled with fear and doubt into a people who worshipped with joy and gratitude. This teaches us that worship is the natural response to witnessing God's deliverance. When we see His power at work in our lives, when we experience His protection and salvation, our hearts are filled with worship. Worship is not something we do out of obligation; it is the outpouring of a heart that has been touched by God's grace and power. The Israelites' journey from weakness to worship is a powerful reminder that our darkest moments can become the backdrop for God's greatest work in our lives. When we witness His deliverance, we are moved to worship, not because we are commanded to, but because we can't help but respond to His goodness.

The transformation from weakness to worship is something that all believers experience at some point in their walk with God. There are moments in life when we feel overwhelmed by our circumstances, when we are keenly aware of our own weakness and inability to change our situation. In those moments, it is easy to feel defeated, to wonder if God sees us or cares about what we are going through. But the story of the Red Sea reminds us that God is always at work, even when we feel weakest. He is not distant or indifferent to our struggles. He sees our weakness, and He steps into our situation with His strength. And when He delivers us, our weakness is transformed into worship. What once felt like the end becomes the beginning of a deeper relationship with God, one that is built on trust, gratitude, and worship.

This pattern of moving from weakness to worship is not unique to the Israelites at the Red Sea; it is a theme that runs throughout the Bible. We see it in the life of David, who often cried out to God in his moments of weakness but always ended in worship. We see it in the life of Job, who, despite losing everything, declared, "The Lord gave, and the Lord hath taken away; blessed be the name of the Lord" (Job 1:21). We see it in the life of the apostle Paul, who famously wrote, "When I am weak, then am I strong" (2 Corinthians 12:10). These examples teach us that weakness is not something to be feared or avoided; it is often the very place where God's power is most clearly displayed. When we are weak, we are forced to rely on God, and it is in that reliance that we experience His strength and deliverance. And when we witness His deliverance, we are moved to worship Him with hearts that are full of gratitude and awe.

In our own lives, we can take comfort in the fact that God specializes in turning weakness into worship. No matter what we are facing, no matter how impossible our situation may seem, we can trust that God is with us, working behind the scenes to bring about our deliverance. We may not always see the way forward, just as the Israelites couldn't see how they would escape the Egyptians. But just as God parted the Red Sea, making a way where there was no way, He can do the same in our lives. And when He does, our response will be the same as the Israelites: worship. When we witness God's hand at work in our lives, when we see how He has delivered us from our enemies, our hearts will be filled with worship. Weakness is not the end of the story; it is the beginning of a journey that leads to worship.

In conclusion, Exodus 14:21-22, 26-27 teaches us a profound lesson about how God can turn our weakness into worship. The Israelites, who began their journey in fear and doubt, witnessed the miraculous power of God as He parted the Red Sea and wiped out their enemies. This experience transformed them from a people of weakness into a people of worship. Their fear gave way to faith, and their doubt turned into gratitude as they saw God's hand at work. This story reminds us that in our moments of weakness, God is not absent—He is working to bring about our deliverance. And when we witness His salvation, we are moved to worship Him with hearts full of awe and gratitude. Our weakness is not something to be ashamed of; it is the very place where God's strength is made perfect. And when we experience His strength, our natural response is to worship the One who has delivered us.

Chapter 10 - Ways of God Are Our Protection

In Exodus 14:21-22, 26-27, we witness one of the most dramatic and awe-inspiring moments in all of Scripture, a moment that serves as a vivid reminder of how God's ways are our protection. The Israelites, newly freed from the bonds of slavery in Egypt, were faced with a seemingly impossible situation. They were trapped between the Red Sea and the approaching Egyptian army, which was armed with chariots and soldiers—an unstoppable force from a human perspective. The Israelites, vulnerable and without any military strength of their own, saw no way out. They were terrified, feeling weak and hopeless in the face of such overwhelming opposition. Yet, in the midst of this crisis, Moses, under God's direction, stretched out his hand over the sea, and something miraculous happened. The Lord caused a strong east wind to blow all night, parting the waters of the Red Sea and creating a dry path for the Israelites to cross. The waters stood like walls on either side of them, providing not only a way forward but also protection from the enemy behind them. This moment reveals a profound truth: God's ways are not just solutions to our problems; they are the very means by which He protects and delivers us. The Israelites were saved not by their own strength or military might, but by following the path that God had opened for them—a path that no one could have predicted, a way that only God could provide. This teaches us that when we feel trapped, weak, or overwhelmed by life's challenges, the safest and most secure place we can be is walking in God's ways. His ways are our protection, even when the odds seem stacked against us.

The Egyptians, with all their military power, were no match for God's ways. Pharaoh's army, which had enslaved the Israelites for generations and had pursued them relentlessly even after their release, represented the height of human power and arrogance. From a worldly perspective, the Egyptians held all the advantages: they had superior numbers, weaponry, and experience in battle. But despite all this, they were helpless against the power of God. As they pursued the Israelites into the Red Sea, they probably believed that victory was certain. After all, they had the upper hand—or so they thought. What they didn't realize was that the very path they were following, the path that God had opened for the Israelites, was not a path of safety for them. In Exodus 14:26-27, we read how God instructed Moses to stretch out his hand once more, and the waters that had been parted returned to their place, covering the Egyptian chariots and soldiers. "And Moses stretched forth his hand over the sea, and the sea returned to his strength when the morning appeared; and the Egyptians fled against it; and the Lord overthrew the Egyptians in the midst of the sea" (Exodus 14:27). The same waters that had stood as walls of protection for the Israelites became a grave for the Egyptians. This teaches us that God's ways are designed to protect His people, but those who oppose Him will find themselves overthrown by the very forces they thought they could control. No amount of human strength or strategy can stand against the plans and purposes of God.

God's ways are often unexpected, but they are always effective. The parting of the Red Sea was not something the Israelites could have imagined or planned for. From their perspective, the sea represented an impassable barrier, a dead end with no escape. But God's ways are higher than our ways, and His thoughts are higher than our thoughts (Isaiah 55:9). What seems like an obstacle to us is often the very thing God will use to bring about our deliverance. The Red Sea, which had been a source of fear and anxiety for the Israelites, became the means of their salvation. This teaches us that we must trust God's ways, even when they don't make sense to us in the moment. Often, we find ourselves in situations where we feel like we are trapped or overwhelmed by circumstances beyond our control. In those moments, it's easy to question God's plan or to try to find our own way out. But the story of the Red Sea reminds us that God's ways are always the safest path. When we follow Him, He protects us, even when the path seems uncertain or dangerous. The Israelites had to step out in faith, walking between the walls of water, trusting that God would hold them back until they reached the other side. In the same way, we are called to trust God's ways, even when they lead us through difficult or frightening circumstances. His way is always the best way, and His protection is guaranteed for those who follow Him.

One of the most comforting aspects of this story is the reminder that God's protection is not dependent on our strength or ability. The Israelites were weak, both physically and emotionally. They were a group of former slaves, not trained warriors, and they had just come out of a long period of oppression. They had no weapons, no military strategy, and no experience in battle. By all human standards, they were defenseless. But God's protection doesn't require us to be strong; it requires us to trust in His strength. The Israelites didn't need to fight the Egyptians themselves—God fought for them. In Exodus 14:14, Moses tells the people, "The Lord shall fight for you, and ye shall hold your peace." This is a powerful reminder that when we are walking in God's ways, we don't have to rely on our own strength to overcome the challenges we face. God's ways are our protection, and He will fight on our behalf. The Israelites were simply called to walk the path that God had opened for them, and as they did, they experienced His protection in a way that they never could have achieved on their own. This teaches us that our weakness is not a hindrance to God's ability to protect us. In fact, it is often in our weakness that God's strength is most clearly displayed. When we rely on Him and follow His ways, He protects us in ways that far surpass anything we could accomplish in our own strength.

The destruction of the Egyptian army also highlights the completeness of God's protection. When God delivers His people, He doesn't do it halfway. The Israelites were not just saved from immediate danger; their enemies were wiped out completely. Exodus 14:28 tells us, "And the waters returned, and covered the chariots, and the horsemen, and all the host of Pharaoh that came into the sea after them; there remained not so much as one of them." The threat was eliminated entirely. This is a powerful reminder that when God protects us, He does so completely and thoroughly. He doesn't leave any loose ends or lingering threats. The Egyptians, who had oppressed the Israelites for generations, were utterly defeated, and the Israelites were able to continue their journey without fear of being pursued. This teaches us that God's protection is not temporary or partial; it is complete and enduring. When we walk in God's ways, we can trust that He will not only protect us in the moment but will also ensure that the threats we face are dealt with once and for all. This doesn't mean that we will never face challenges again, but it does mean that God's protection is total, and His deliverance is final. The Egyptians, who had seemed so powerful and unstoppable, were no match for God's ways, and their defeat was a testimony to the fact that no enemy is too great for God to overcome.

The parting of the Red Sea also teaches us that God's protection often requires us to wait on Him and trust in His timing. The Israelites were in a desperate situation, and it would have been easy for them to panic and try to find their own way out. But Moses told them to "stand still, and see the salvation of the Lord" (Exodus 14:13). Sometimes, the hardest thing to do in the face of danger is to wait and trust in God's plan. We often want immediate solutions, quick fixes, and instant deliverance. But God's ways are not rushed. The Bible tells us that the wind blew all night, pushing the waters back and drying the ground for the Israelites to walk on. This was not an instant miracle; it took time. The Israelites had to wait, trusting that God was at work even when they couldn't see the full picture. This teaches us that God's protection often involves a process, and we must be willing to wait on His timing. When we are in the midst of a crisis, it can be difficult to wait on God, especially when the enemy seems to be closing in. But the story of the Red Sea reminds us that God's timing is perfect, and His ways are always the safest path. When we wait on Him, we are protected, even when it feels like we are surrounded by danger. God's protection is not dependent on our ability to act quickly or decisively; it is dependent on our willingness to trust Him and wait for His deliverance.

The story of the Red Sea is also a powerful reminder of God's faithfulness to His promises. God had promised to deliver the Israelites from slavery in Egypt, and although their journey to freedom was filled with challenges, God remained faithful to His word. The parting of the Red Sea was not just a moment of protection; it was a fulfillment of God's promise to lead His people to freedom. This teaches us that God's protection is not arbitrary or random; it is rooted in His covenant faithfulness. When we walk in God's ways, we can trust that He will protect us because He has promised to do so. The Israelites were able to walk through the waters because God had made a way for them, and He had promised to bring them safely to the other side. In the same way, when we face challenges or threats in our own lives, we can hold on to the promises of God, knowing that He is faithful to protect us and to guide us through. His ways are always the safest path because they are grounded in His unchanging character and His unwavering commitment to His people.

In conclusion, Exodus 14:21-22, 26-27 teaches us the profound truth that God's ways are our protection. The Israelites, trapped between the Red Sea and the Egyptian army, were in a position of weakness and fear. But God made a way for them, parting the waters and providing a path of safety through what seemed like an impossible situation. As they followed God's way, they experienced His protection in a way that far surpassed anything they could have imagined. The Egyptians, despite their military might, were no match for God's ways, and they were wiped out completely when they attempted to follow the same path. This story reminds us that when we walk in God's ways, we are protected, even when the odds seem stacked against us. God's protection is not dependent on our strength or ability; it is rooted in His power and His faithfulness. When we trust in His ways and wait on His timing, we experience the fullness of His protection, and we see His deliverance in ways that leave no doubt about His sovereignty and care for His people. God's ways are always the safest path, and when we walk in them, we can rest in the assurance that we are under His protection, no matter what challenges we face.

Chapter 11 - Witness to God's Glory

In Exodus 14:21-22, 26-27, we are given one of the most awe-inspiring and unforgettable moments in the entire Bible: the parting of the Red Sea. This event stands as one of the most powerful demonstrations of God's glory and might, a moment that not only saved the Israelites but also became a lasting testimony of God's greatness for generations to come. The Red Sea parting was not just a miracle of physical deliverance but a divine spectacle that revealed the unmatched power and authority of God over creation. It was a moment that displayed His ability to control the very elements of nature, and it revealed His glory in a way that no human could ever achieve. The Israelites were trapped between the sea and the approaching Egyptian army, who were armed with chariots and all the military might of one of the most powerful empires of that time. From a human standpoint, the Israelites had no way out. Their situation seemed hopeless, and fear gripped their hearts as they faced what appeared to be certain destruction. But it was in this moment of desperation that God chose to reveal His glory. He instructed Moses to stretch out his hand over the sea, and as Moses obeyed, the Lord sent a strong east wind that blew all night, causing the sea to part and creating dry land for the Israelites to walk through. The waters formed walls on either side of them, standing tall and still as the Israelites made their way across. This was not just a small miracle—it was a monumental display of God's power, a moment where the natural laws of the world were suspended by the divine will of God. The parting of the Red Sea was an undeniable witness to God's glory, a powerful reminder that He is sovereign over all creation and that His power knows no limits.

The Red Sea parting was more than just a means of escape for the Israelites; it was an event that left no doubt about the greatness of God. It was a clear and visible manifestation of His ability to control the forces of nature, to intervene in human history, and to work miracles that defy all human understanding. The sheer scale of the miracle was overwhelming. Imagine the scene: the sea, which had once seemed like an impassable barrier, was now split down the middle, with the waters held back by nothing but the power of God. The Israelites walked through on dry ground, surrounded by towering walls of water on either side. This event was not just about physical salvation—it was about showing the world who God is. The Israelites, who had cried out in fear just moments before, were now witnesses to the glory of God in action. This moment became a turning point for them, a moment where they could no longer doubt the power and presence of the God who had delivered them from slavery. It was a moment that called for worship and reverence because they had seen, firsthand, the glory of God displayed in a way that no one could ignore.

This story teaches us that when God works in our lives, it is not only for our benefit but also as a witness to His glory. The parting of the Red Sea was a public display of God's greatness, a moment that not only saved His people but also demonstrated His power to the Egyptians, the Israelites, and to all who would hear of it. God's glory was revealed in such a way that no one could deny His involvement. The Egyptians, who had believed themselves to be invincible, were humbled by this display of divine power. Their chariots and soldiers, which had been symbols of their military might, were no match for the God of Israel. When God closed the waters over them, drowning the entire Egyptian army, it became clear that no human force could stand against God's will. This was a definitive witness to God's glory, showing that He is the ultimate authority over all nations, all armies, and all people. The parting of the Red Sea became a lasting testimony of God's power, one that would be remembered and retold for generations as a reminder of His greatness.

The parting of the Red Sea also reveals the relationship between God's glory and His deliverance of His people. The Israelites were in a position of weakness and vulnerability, unable to save themselves from the Egyptian army that was closing in on them. But in their moment of need, God stepped in and provided a way where there was no way. This act of deliverance was not only a demonstration of God's love and care for His people but also a way to reveal His glory. God's glory is often revealed most clearly in our moments of greatest need, when we are powerless to save ourselves and must rely entirely on His intervention. The Israelites could do nothing to escape their situation on their own, but God made a way through the sea, and in doing so, He revealed His power in a way that left no doubt about His greatness. This teaches us that when we witness God's deliverance in our own lives, it is a moment to recognize His glory. It is a moment to realize that His power is far greater than anything we can imagine, and that He is worthy of our worship and praise. God's glory is not just an abstract concept; it is something that we can witness in the real, tangible ways He works in our lives.

As we reflect on the parting of the Red Sea, we see that God's glory is not limited to the miraculous. It is revealed in the everyday ways that He guides and protects His people. The pillar of cloud by day and the pillar of fire by night were constant reminders of God's presence with the Israelites throughout their journey. These visible signs of God's glory provided guidance and protection, showing the Israelites that God was with them every step of the way. While the parting of the Red Sea was a dramatic and unforgettable moment, the pillars of cloud and fire were ongoing witnesses to God's glory. They reminded the Israelites that God's presence was not just something that appeared in moments of crisis but was with them always. This teaches us that God's glory is not only revealed in the big, miraculous moments but also in the quiet, steady presence of God in our lives. His glory is seen in the ways He leads us, protects us, and provides for us day by day. We may not always witness the dramatic parting of a sea, but we can witness God's glory in the way He is present with us in the ordinary moments of life, guiding us through every situation.

The story of the Red Sea also teaches us that when we witness God's glory, our response should be one of worship. After the Israelites crossed the Red Sea and saw the Egyptian army destroyed, their immediate response was to worship. In Exodus 15, we see the song of Moses and the Israelites, a song of praise and thanksgiving for God's deliverance. "Then sang Moses and the children of Israel this song unto the Lord, and spake, saying, I will sing unto the Lord, for he hath triumphed gloriously: the horse and his rider hath he thrown into the sea" (Exodus 15:1). This song is a beautiful expression of worship in response to witnessing God's glory. The Israelites had seen firsthand the power and greatness of God, and their hearts were filled with gratitude and awe. This teaches us that when we witness God's glory in our own lives—whether through His provision, protection, or deliverance—our response should be to worship Him. Worship is the natural response to witnessing God's greatness. It is an acknowledgment that He is worthy of all honor and praise because of who He is and what He has done. When we see God at work in our lives, our hearts should overflow with worship, just as the hearts of the Israelites did after they crossed the Red Sea.

The parting of the Red Sea was also a witness to the surrounding nations of God's glory. As the news of this miraculous event spread, it became clear to other nations that the God of Israel was not like the gods of Egypt or the gods of the other peoples of the ancient world. The power displayed at the Red Sea was unparalleled, and it sent a message to the surrounding nations that the God of Israel was the true God, the One who had control over the seas and the elements of nature. This teaches us that when God works in our lives, it can become a witness to others of His glory. When people see the ways that God provides for us, protects us, and delivers us from difficult situations, it can point them to the greatness of God. Our lives can become a testimony of God's glory, showing others that He is real, that He is powerful, and that He is worthy of their worship as well. The parting of the Red Sea was not just for the Israelites—it was a moment that revealed God's glory to the world, and it serves as a reminder that our own experiences of God's power can be a witness to those around us.

Moreover, the parting of the Red Sea demonstrates that God's glory is not dependent on human effort. The Israelites were powerless to part the sea on their own, and they were powerless to defeat the Egyptian army. Their salvation came entirely from God. This teaches us that God's glory is revealed not through our strength or abilities but through His sovereign power. We do not earn or create the miracles that happen in our lives—God, in His grace and mercy, acts on our behalf, and His glory is revealed when we recognize that He is the source of our deliverance. The Israelites had no choice but to trust in God's plan, and when they did, they witnessed a miracle that was far beyond anything they could have imagined. This reminds us that when we trust in God and rely on His strength rather than our own, we open the door for His glory to be revealed in our lives. God's glory is most clearly seen when we acknowledge that He is the one in control, and that it is by His power, not ours, that we are saved.

The parting of the Red Sea also serves as a reminder that God's glory is revealed not only in moments of victory but also in moments of judgment. The same waters that provided a path of salvation for the Israelites became the means of destruction for the Egyptian army. God's glory was revealed not only in the deliverance of His people but also in the judgment of their enemies. This teaches us that God's glory encompasses both His mercy and His justice. He is a

God who saves, but He is also a God who judges. The Egyptians had oppressed the Israelites for generations, and their refusal to acknowledge God's authority led to their downfall. This aspect of God's glory reminds us that He is holy and righteous, and that His judgments are just. When we witness God's glory, we are reminded not only of His love and mercy but also of His power and authority over all creation. God's glory is revealed in both His ability to save and His right to judge.

In conclusion, Exodus 14:21-22, 26-27 reveals the incredible glory and power of God through the parting of the Red Sea. This event was a powerful witness to God's sovereignty over creation, His ability to deliver His people, and His authority over all nations. The parting of the Red Sea was not only a moment of physical salvation for the Israelites but also a revelation of God's glory, a reminder that He is the one true God who is worthy of worship and praise. As the Israelites witnessed God's glory in action, their fear turned to faith, and their weakness turned to worship. This story teaches us that when we witness God's work in our lives, whether through miracles, provision, protection, or deliverance, it is a call to worship Him and to recognize His greatness. God's glory is not something that is limited to the pages of Scripture—it is something that we can witness in our own lives as we experience His power and presence. And when we witness God's glory, our response should be one of worship, gratitude, and awe, as we acknowledge that He is the source of all that is good and that He alone is worthy of our praise. The parting of the Red Sea stands as an eternal witness to God's glory, a reminder that He is always at work, revealing His greatness to His people and to the world.

Chapter 12 - Water Becomes a Way of Deliverance

In Exodus 14:21-22, 26-27, one of the most extraordinary and miraculous moments in biblical history unfolds before us—the parting of the Red Sea. This moment is not only a demonstration of God's immense power but also a powerful illustration of how the very things we often perceive as obstacles can become the means of our deliverance when we trust in God's will. The Israelites, having been freed from slavery in Egypt, found themselves in a seemingly impossible situation. They were trapped between the Red Sea on one side and the approaching Egyptian army on the other. From a human perspective, the situation was hopeless. The waters of the sea represented an insurmountable barrier, and the Egyptians, with their chariots and soldiers, were closing in, threatening to destroy them or drag them back into captivity. Panic and fear swept through the Israelite camp as they cried out, questioning whether their escape from Egypt had led them to an even more terrifying end. But it was in this moment of desperation and fear that God chose to act in a way that no one could have predicted. What the Israelites saw as an obstacle—the vast, seemingly impassable waters of the Red Sea—became the very path through which God would deliver them. God instructed Moses to stretch out his hand over the sea, and as Moses obeyed, a strong east wind blew all night, parting the waters and creating a dry path for the Israelites to walk through. The waters, which had once seemed to be a barrier, now stood as walls on either side of the Israelites, providing protection as they made their way to safety. This story teaches us a profound lesson: the very things we often perceive as barriers in our lives—those overwhelming obstacles that seem impossible to overcome—can be transformed into the path of our deliverance when we place our trust in God and His will.

The parting of the Red Sea is not just a story about physical deliverance; it is a vivid representation of the spiritual journey that many of us go through. The waters of the Red Sea, which initially seemed to be a symbol of defeat and death, became a symbol of salvation and life. The Israelites, facing what they believed to be certain destruction, were led by God through the very waters they feared. This teaches us that what we perceive as our greatest challenges or obstacles can, in God's hands, become the means through which we are delivered and brought into a new phase of life. The key lies in trusting God's plan, even when the way forward seems unclear or impossible. The Israelites had no way of knowing how they would escape their situation, but they were called to trust that God had a plan, even when they couldn't see it. In the same way, we are often faced with situations in life that seem insurmountable—whether it's a difficult relationship, a financial crisis, a health issue, or a personal failure. In these moments, it's easy to see the obstacle as something that will defeat us. But the story of the Red Sea reminds us that God is able to take those very obstacles and turn them into the path of our deliverance.

God's intervention at the Red Sea also teaches us about His ability to make a way where there seems to be no way. The Israelites were trapped, with no apparent options for escape. To their eyes, the waters of the Red Sea were an impossible barrier, and the Egyptian army was a looming threat. But God is not limited by the same boundaries that we see. What seems impossible to us is entirely possible for God. In Isaiah 55:8-9, God says, "For my thoughts are not your thoughts, neither are your ways my ways... For as the heavens are higher than the earth, so are my ways higher than your ways, and my thoughts than your thoughts." This passage reflects the reality that God often works in ways that we cannot predict or understand, but His ways are always perfect. The parting of the Red Sea was an event that defied human logic and understanding, yet it was God's way of delivering His people. This teaches us that we should never limit God's ability to work in our lives based on what we think is possible. He is the Creator of the universe, the One who holds the seas in His hands, and He can turn even the most impossible situations into a means of deliverance. The Red Sea, which had seemed like an impassable wall, was transformed into a pathway, showing that God's ways are always higher and greater than anything we can imagine.

The transformation of the waters from a barrier to a path of deliverance also symbolizes how God can take the very things that we fear and turn them into instruments of His grace and salvation. The Israelites were terrified of the waters, as they represented an impassable obstacle that could have led to their destruction. Yet, in God's hands, those same waters became a shield and a way of escape. This teaches us that the things we fear the most—whether they are external challenges or internal struggles—can be used by God to bring about our deliverance. Fear has a way of magnifying obstacles, making them seem larger and more powerful than they really are. But when we place our trust in God, He has the power to diminish those fears and show us that He is greater than anything we face. The waters of the Red Sea, which had once inspired fear and hopelessness, were transformed into a symbol of God's protection and salvation. This teaches us that when we place our trust in God, even the things that seem most threatening or overwhelming can be turned into instruments of His grace.

Furthermore, the parting of the Red Sea illustrates the importance of faith in the process of deliverance. The Israelites had to take a step of faith by walking into the path that God had created through the waters. It must have been a daunting experience to walk between the walls of water, not knowing how long they would remain parted or what might happen as they journeyed through. Yet, they were called to trust that God, who had parted the waters, would keep them held back until they reached the other side. This teaches us that deliverance often requires us to step out in faith, even when we don't see the full picture or know how everything will work out. Faith is not about having all the answers or knowing the outcome—it's about trusting that God is in control and that He will lead us safely through whatever obstacles we face. Just as the Israelites had to walk through the waters in faith, we are often called to walk through challenging circumstances with the assurance that God is with us and that He will guide us safely to the other side.

In Exodus 14:26-27, we see the culmination of God's deliverance as He instructs Moses to stretch out his hand over the sea once more, and the waters return to their place, covering the Egyptian army. "And Moses stretched forth his hand over the sea, and the sea returned to his strength when the morning appeared; and the Egyptians fled against it; and the Lord overthrew the Egyptians in the midst of the sea." The same waters that had been a path of salvation for the Israelites became a means of judgment for the Egyptians. This teaches us that God's deliverance is not only about saving His people but also about bringing justice and defeating the forces that seek to harm us. The Egyptians, who had enslaved the Israelites for generations, were pursuing them with the intent to bring them back into captivity. But God, in His justice, used the waters of the Red Sea to bring an end to their oppression. This reminds us that when God delivers us, He doesn't just bring us out of danger—He also deals with the forces that have been working against us. The Egyptians, who had seemed so powerful and unstoppable, were completely wiped out by the waters, showing that no enemy is too great for God to defeat.

The parting of the Red Sea also reveals the completeness of God's deliverance. When God saves, He does so fully and completely. The Israelites were not just temporarily saved from the Egyptian army; their enemies were completely destroyed, and they were free to continue their journey to the Promised Land without fear of being pursued. This teaches us that when God delivers us, He doesn't leave the job half-done. He completes the work of salvation, ensuring that the things that once threatened us are no longer a danger. The waters that had seemed like an obstacle were transformed into a symbol of God's total victory over the enemies of His people. This serves as a reminder that when we place our trust in God, He not only delivers us from immediate danger but also brings about a complete and final victory over the forces that seek to harm us.

The story of the Red Sea also teaches us about the importance of obedience in the process of deliverance. Moses obeyed God's command to stretch out his hand over the sea, and it was through his obedience that the miracle took place. This teaches us that obedience to God's instructions is often the key to experiencing His deliverance. The Israelites, too, had to obey God's command to walk through the sea on the dry ground that He had provided. They could have chosen to stay where they were, paralyzed by fear, but instead, they stepped forward in obedience and faith. This teaches us that when God opens a path of deliverance for us, we must be willing to step forward in faith and obedience. Deliverance is not something that happens passively—it requires us to actively trust God and follow the path He has laid out for us, even when it seems uncertain or difficult.

The parting of the Red Sea is also a reminder of God's faithfulness to His promises. God had promised to deliver the Israelites from slavery and lead them to the Promised Land, and the parting of the Red Sea was a critical step in the fulfillment of that promise. This teaches us that God is always faithful to His word, even when the way forward seems impossible. The Israelites had no way of crossing the Red Sea on their own, but God made a way because He had promised to deliver them. This reminds us that we can trust in God's promises, even when we can't see how they will be fulfilled. God is always faithful, and He will make a way for us, even when we face seemingly insurmountable obstacles.

In conclusion, the parting of the Red Sea in Exodus 14:21-22, 26-27 is a powerful illustration of how God can turn what seems like an overwhelming obstacle into the very means of our deliverance. The waters of the Red Sea, which had once represented fear, danger, and impossibility, were transformed into a path of salvation for the Israelites. This story teaches us that when we trust in God's will and follow His ways, the barriers we face can be turned into opportunities for His deliverance. The Red Sea, which had once seemed like a dead end, became the way forward, showing that God's power is greater than any obstacle we face. Whether we are facing personal challenges, fears, or seemingly insurmountable difficulties, the story of the Red Sea reminds us that God can make a way where there seems to be no way. When we place our trust in Him, He can take the very things that we fear and use them to bring about our salvation. And when He delivers us, He does so completely, ensuring that the forces that once threatened us are defeated and that we are free to continue our journey in faith and trust in His plan. The parting of the Red Sea stands as a timeless reminder that with God, nothing is impossible, and that the waters we once feared can become the way of our deliverance when we trust in His will.

Conclusion

As we conclude "Walking Through Walls: God's Power to Part the Storms of Life", we are reminded that the story of the Red Sea is not just a historical account but a powerful message for every believer today. Just as the Israelites faced what seemed like an insurmountable obstacle, we, too, encounter moments in life when the challenges before us appear overwhelming. Whether it's financial hardship, relational struggles, health crises, or personal failures, these moments can leave us feeling trapped, as if there is no way out. But just as God made a way for His people through the waters of the Red Sea, He promises to do the same for us. The same God who parted the sea, creating a path of deliverance for His people, is at work in our lives today, turning what seems like impossible barriers into opportunities for His glory.

God's faithfulness is not bound by the circumstances that surround us. He remains sovereign over every storm, every obstacle, and every trial we face. Through the story of the Red Sea, we see His perfect timing, His unwavering protection, and His ability to turn impossible situations into pathways of deliverance. This is not just a story of God's power over nature—it is a testament to His love for His people and His desire to see them through to the other side of every struggle. God's timing may not always align with our own, but He is always working, always moving on our behalf, and always faithful to His promises.

As Christians, the challenge before us is to continue walking in faith, even when the way forward seems unclear. Just as the Israelites had to trust God and step forward into the parted waters, we are called to trust God's leading, even when the path seems uncertain. Faith is not about seeing the whole plan laid out before us—it's about trusting that God is in control and that He will provide a way through every trial. It's about obedience, patience, and surrendering our fears and anxieties to the One who holds the seas in His hands. When we walk in obedience, trusting in God's timing and His plan, we position ourselves to witness His power and His glory in our lives.

Let this story of the Red Sea be a continual reminder that no obstacle is too great for God. When you feel trapped, when the waves seem too high, and when the barriers appear impenetrable, remember that God is the One who makes the impossible possible. He is the God who parts the waters, and He is the God who goes before you, making a way through the storms of life. As you move forward in your walk with the Lord, keep trusting, keep walking, and keep believing that with God, all things are possible. Stand firm in faith, knowing that the same God who delivered the Israelites from the hands of the Egyptians is with you, guiding you, protecting you, and leading you to victory. Let your life be a witness to His power and glory as you continue walking through the walls that once seemed impossible to pass.

Don't miss out!

Visit the website below and you can sign up to receive emails whenever Joshua Rhoades publishes a new book. There's no charge and no obligation.

https://books2read.com/r/B-A-AJLBB-SJNAF

BOOKS 2 READ

Connecting independent readers to independent writers.

Did you love *Walking Through Walls God's Power to Part the Storms of Life*?
Then you should read *Biblical Counsel on Anger*[1] by Joshua Rhoades!

[2]

Anger is something we all experience at some point in our lives. It's a powerful emotion that can sometimes lead us to say or do things we later regret. However, anger itself isn't necessarily wrong—it's a natural reaction to feeling hurt, wronged, or frustrated. The real challenge lies in how we manage that anger. If not controlled, anger can become destructive, damaging relationships, leading to poor decisions, and distancing us from the peace and joy that God desires for us. The Bible offers abundant wisdom on how to handle anger in a way that honors God and promotes spiritual growth. **Biblical Counsel on Anger** is a book dedicated to exploring what Scripture teaches about this intense emotion, providing practical guidance for managing it in our daily lives. In this book, we delve into key Bible passages that address the nature of anger—teaching us how to be slow to anger, how to differentiate between righteous and sinful anger, and how to respond with patience, forgiveness, and love when we're provoked. We'll also examine the consequences of letting anger control us and the hope and healing that come from following God's path. Whether you struggle with anger yourself, want to help someone else, or seek a deeper understanding of this emotion from a biblical perspective, this book offers wisdom and practical tools grounded in God's Word. The teachings of

---

1. https://books2read.com/u/38GBKO

2. https://books2read.com/u/38GBKO

the Bible on anger are as relevant today as they were thousands of years ago. By aligning your responses to anger with God's guidance, you can break free from the hold of this powerful emotion, find greater peace, and build healthier, more loving relationships. As you read through **Biblical Counsel on Anger**, I encourage you to approach each page with an open heart, ready to learn, grow, and be transformed by the timeless wisdom of Scripture.